Karl Marx

Karl Marx

By
P. K Das
M. K. Singh

MP

MAHAVEE**R**
PUBLISHERS

Published by
MAHAVEER PUBLISHERS
4764/2A, 23-Ansari Road, Daryaganj
New Delhi – 110002
Ph. : 011 – 66629669–79–89
e-mail : mahaveerpublishers@gmail.com

© Mahaveer Publishers

First Edition : January 2013
Second Edition : 2015

Karl Marx
ISBN : 9789350880081

Distributed in India by
VAIBHAV BOOK SERVICE
e-mail : vaibhavbookservice@gmail.com

Distributed in Nepal by
BAJRANGBALI BOOK ENTERPRISES PVT. LTD.
Jyatha Mushyabahal, Ward No. 27, Kathmandu, Nepal
e-mail : bajrangbalibooks@gmail.com

Printed in India

Introduction

Karl Heinrich Marx was a German philosopher, political economist, historian, sociologist, humanist, political theorist and revolutionary credited as the founder of communism.

Marx's approach to history and politics is indicated by the opening line of the first chapter of *The Communist Manifesto* (1848): "The history of all hitherto existing society is the history of class struggles." Marx argued that capitalism, like previous socioeconomic systems, will produce internal tensions which will lead to its destruction. Just as capitalism replaced feudalism, capitalism itself will be displaced by communism, a classless society which emerges after a transitional period, socialism, in which the state would be nothing else but the revolutionary dictatorship of the proletariat.

On the one hand, Marx argued for a systemic understanding of socioeconomic change, he argued that it is the structural contradictions within capitalism which necessitate its end, giving way to communism:

"The development of Modern Industry, therefore, cuts from under its feet the very foundation on which the bourgeoisie produces and appropriates products. What the bourgeoisie, therefore, produces, above all, are its own grave-diggers. Its fall and the victory of the proletariat are equally inevitable."

- (The Communist Manifesto)

On the other hand, Marx argued that socioeconomic change occurred through organized revolutionary action. He argued that capitalism will end through the organized actions of an international working class, led by a Communist Party: "Communism is for us not a state of affairs which is to be established, an ideal to which reality [will] have to adjust itself. We call communism the real movement which abolishes the present state of things. The conditions of this movement result from the premises now in existence." (From *The German Ideology*)

While Marx was a relatively obscure figure in his own lifetime, his ideas began to exert a major influence on workers' movements shortly after his death. This influence was given added impetus by the victory of the Marxist Bolsheviks in the Russian October Revolution, and there are few parts of the world which were not significantly touched by Marxian ideas in the course of the twentieth century.

Contents

1

Biography

Karl Heinrich Marx was born in Trier, in the Kingdom of Prussia's Province of the Lower Rhine and the third of seven children. His father, Heinrich Marx (1777-1838), born Herschel Mordechai, the son of Levy Mordechai (1743-1804) and Eva Lwow (1753-1823), was descended from a long line of rabbis but converted to Lutheran Christianity, despite his many deistic tendencies and his admiration of such Enlightenment figures as Voltaire and Rousseau, in order to be allowed to practice Law. Marx's mother was Henriette née Pressburg (1788-1863). His siblings were Sophie (d. 1883) (m. Wilhelm Robert Schmalhausen), Hermann (1819-1842), Henriette (1820-1856), Louise (1821-1893) (m. Johann Carel Juta), Emilie, Caroline (1824-1847) and Eduard (1834-1837). His mother was the grand-aunt of industrialists Gerard Philips and Anton Philips and a maternal descendant of the Barent-Cohen family through her parents Isaac Heijmans Presburg (Presburg, c. 1747 - Nijmegen, May 3, 1832) and wife Nanette Salomon Barent-Cohen (Amsterdam, c. 1764 - Nijmegen, April 7, 1833), the daughter of Salomon David Barent-Cohen (d. 1807) and wife Sara Brandes, in turn the uncle and aunt by marriage of Nathan Mayer Rothschild's wife.

Soon after losing his job as editor of *Rheinische Zeitung*, a Cologne newspaper, Karl Marx was married to Jenny von Westphalen, the educated daughter of a Prussian baron, on June 19, 1843 in Kreuznacher Pauluskirche, Bad Kreuznach. Their engagement was kept secret at first, and for several years was opposed by both the Marxes and Westphalens. From 1844 to 1848, Marx enjoyed a very comfortable lifestyle, with income derived from the sale of his works, his salary, gifts from friends and allies; a large inheritance from his father's death, long delayed, also became available in March 1848. During the first half of the 1850s the Marx family lived in poverty and constant fear of creditors in a three room flat on Dean Street in Soho, London. Marx and Jenny already had four children and three more were to follow. Of these only three survived to adulthood. Marx's major source of income at this time was Engels, who was drawing a steadily increasing income from the family business in Manchester. This was supplemented by weekly articles written as a foreign correspondent for the *New York Daily Tribune*. Inheritances from one of Jenny's uncles and her mother who died in 1856 allowed the family to move to somewhat more salubrious lodgings at 9, *Grafton Terrace*, Kentish Town a new suburb on the then-outskirts of London. Marx generally lived a hand-to-mouth existence, forever at the limits of his resources, although this did to some extent depend upon his spending on relatively bourgeois luxuries, which he felt were necessities for his wife and children given their social status and the mores of the time.

Marx's children by his wife were: Jenny Caroline (m. Longuet; 1844-1883); Jenny Laura (m. Lafargue; 1845-1911); Edgar (1847-1855); Henry Edward Guy ("Guido;" 1849-1850); Jenny Eveline Frances ("Franziska:" 1851-1852); Jenny Julia Eleanor (1855-1898); and one more who died before being named (July 1857).

Following the death of his wife Jenny in December 1881, Marx developed a catarrh that kept him in ill health for the last fifteen months of his life. It eventually brought on the bronchitis and pleurisy that killed him in London on March 14, 1883. He died a stateless person and was buried in Highgate Cemetery, London, on March 17, 1883. The messages carved on Marx's tombstone are: "WORKERS OF ALL LANDS UNITE," the final line of The Communist Manifesto, and Engels' version of the 11th *Thesis on Feuerbach:*

"THE PHILOSOPHERS HAVE ONLY
INTERPRETED THE WORLD IN
VARIOUS WAYS - THE POINT
HOWEVER IS TO CHANGE IT"

The tombstone was a monument built in 1954 by the Communist Party of Great Britain with a portrait bust by Laurence Bradshaw; Marx's original tomb had been humbly adorned. In 1970, there was an unsuccessful attempt to destroy the monument, with a homemade bomb.

Several of Marx's closest friends spoke at his funeral, including Wilhelm Liebknecht and Friedrich Engels. Engels' speech included the words:

"On the 14th of March, at a quarter to three in the afternoon, the greatest living thinker ceased to think. He had been left alone for scarcely two minutes, and when we came back we found him in his armchair, peacefully gone to sleep - but forever."

In addition to Engels and Liebknecht, Marx's daughter Eleanor and Charles Longuet and Paul Lafargue, Marx's two French socialist sons-in-law, also attended his funeral. Liebknecht, a founder and leader of the German Social-Democratic Party, gave a speech in German, and Longuet, a prominent figure in the French working-class movement, gave a short statement in French. Two telegrams from workers' parties in France and Spain were also read out. Together with Engels' speech, this was the entire programme of the funeral. Also attending the funeral was Friedrich Lessner, who had been sentenced to three years in prison at the Cologne communist trial of 1852; G. Lochner, who was described by Engels as "an old member of the Communist League" and Carl Schorlemmer, a professor of chemistry in Manchester, a member of the Royal Society, but also an old communist associate of Marx and Engels. Three others attended the funeral - Ray Lankester, Sir John Noe and Leonard Church - making eleven in all.

Marx's daughter Eleanor became a socialist like her father and helped edit his works. Karl Marx was known to become the first major social theorist to form a series of concepts within the break between modern and pre-modern societies.

⊛　⊛　⊛

2

Career

Education

Marx was educated at home until the age of thirteen. After graduating from the Trier Gymnasium, Marx enrolled in the University of Bonn in 1835 at the age of seventeen; he wished to study philosophy and literature, but his father insisted that it was more practical to study law. At Bonn he joined the Trier Tavern Club drinking society and at one point served as its president. Because of Marx's poor grades, his father forced him to transfer to the far more serious and academically oriented Humboldt-Universität in Berlin. During this period, Marx wrote many poems and essays concerning life, using the theological language acquired from his liberal, deistic father, such as "the Deity," but also absorbed the atheistic philosophy of the Young Hegelians who were prominent in Berlin at the time. Marx earned a doctorate in 1841 with a thesis titled *The Difference Between the Democritean and Epicurean Philosophy of Nature*, but he had to submit his dissertation to the University of Jena as he was warned that his reputation among the faculty as a Young Hegelian radical would lead to a poor reception in Berlin.

Marx and the Young Hegelians

The Left, or Young Hegelians, consisted of a group of philosophers and journalists circling around Ludwig Feuerbach and Bruno Bauer opposing their teacher Hegel. Despite their criticism of Hegel's metaphysical assumptions, they made use of Hegel's dialectical method as a powerful weapon for the critique of established religion and politics. One of them, Max Stirner, turned critically against both Feuerbach and Bauer in his book "Der Einzige und sein Eigenthum" (1845, *The Ego and Its Own*), calling these atheists "pious people" for their reification of abstract concepts. Marx, at that time a follower of Feuerbach, was deeply impressed by the work and abandoned Feuerbachian materialism and accomplished what recent authors have denoted as an "epistemological break." He developed the basic concept of historical materialism against Stirner in his book, "Die Deutsche Ideologie" (1846, *The German Ideology*), which he did not publish. Another link to the Young Hegelians was Moses Hess, with whom Marx eventually disagreed, yet to whom he owed many of his insights into the relationship between state, society and religion.

Marx in Paris and Brussels

Towards the end of October 1843, Marx arrived in Paris, France. Paris at this time was the home and headquarters to armies of German, British, Polish, and Italian revolutionaries. Marx, for his part, had come to Paris to work with Arnold Ruge, another revolutionary from Germany, on the *Deutsch-Französische Jahrbücher*. There, on August 28, 1844, at the Café de la Régence on the Place du Palais he met Friedrich Engels, who was to become his most important friend and life-long collaborator. Engels had met Marx only once before and briefly at the office of the *Rheinische Zeitung* in 1842; he went to Paris to show Marx his recently published book, *The Condition of the Working Class in England* in 1844. It was this book that convinced Marx that the working class would be the agent and instrument of the final revolution in history.

After the failure of the *Deutsch-Französische Jahrbücher*, Marx, living on the Rue Vaneau, wrote for the most radical of all German newspapers in Paris, indeed in Europe, the *Vorwärts*, established and run by the secret society called *League of the Just*. When not writing, Marx studied the history of the French Revolution and read Proudhon. He also spent considerable time studying a side of life he had never been acquainted with before-a large urban proletariat.

He re-evaluated his relationship with the Young Hegelians, and as a reply to Bauer's atheism wrote *On the Jewish Question*. This essay was mostly a critique of current notions of civil and human rights and political emancipation, which also included several critical references to Judaism as well as Christianity from a standpoint of social emancipation. Engels, a committed communist, kindled Marx's interest in the situation of the working class and guided Marx's interest in economics. Marx became a communist and set down his views in a series of writings known as the 'Economic and Philosophical Manuscripts of 1844,' which remained unpublished until the 1930s. In the Manuscripts, Marx outlined a humanist conception of communism, influenced by the philosophy of Ludwig Feuerbach and based on a contrast between the alienated nature of labour under capitalism and a communist society in which human beings freely developed their nature in cooperative production.

In January 1845, after *Vorwärts* expressed its hearty approval of the assassination attempt on Frederick William IV, King of Prussia, Marx, among many others, were ordered to leave Paris. He and Engels moved on to Brussels, Belgium.

Marx devoted himself to an intensive study of history and in collaboration with Engels elaborated on his idea of historical materialism, particularly in a manuscript (published posthumously as *The German Ideology*), the basic thesis of which was that "the nature of individuals depends on the material conditions determining their production." Marx traced the history of the various modes of production and predicted the collapse of the present one-industrial capitalism-and its replacement by communism. This was the first major work of what scholars consider to be his later phase, abandoning the Feuerbach-influenced humanism of his earlier work.

Next, Marx wrote *The Poverty of Philosophy* (1847), a response to Pierre-Joseph Proudhon's The Philosophy of Poverty and a critique of French socialist thought. These works laid the foundation for Marx and Engels' most famous work, *The Communist Manifesto*, first published on February 21, 1848, as the manifesto of the Communist League, a small group of European communists who had come to be influenced by Marx and Engels. Later that year, Europe experienced tremendous revolutionary upheaval; Marx was arrested and expelled from Belgium.

In the meantime a radical movement had seized power from King Louis-Philippe in France, and invited Marx to return to Paris, where he witnessed the revolutionary June Days Uprising first hand. When this collapsed in 1849, Marx moved back to Cologne and started the *Neue Rheinische Zeitung* ("New Rhenish Newspaper)." During its existence he was put on trial twice, on February 7, 1849 because of a press misdemeanour, and on the 8th charged with incitement to armed rebellion; both times he was acquitted. The paper was soon suppressed and Marx returned to Paris, but was forced out again; this time he sought refuge in London.

London

Marx moved to London in May 1849, where he was to remain for the rest of his life. For the first few years there, he and his family lived in extreme poverty, which is believed to have acutely damaged Marx's health and shortened his life. He briefly worked as correspondent for the New York Tribune in 1851. In London Marx devoted himself to two activities: revolutionary organizing, and an attempt to understand political economy and capitalism. Having read Engels' study of the working class, Marx turned away from philosophy and devoted himself to the First International, to whose General Council he was elected at its inception in 1864. He was particularly active in preparing for the annual Congresses of the International and leading the struggle against the anarchist wing led by Mikhail Bakunin (1814-1876). Although Marx won this contest, the transfer of the seat of the General Council from London to New York in 1872, which Marx supported, led to the decline of the International. The most important political event during the existence of the International was the *Paris Commune* of 1871 when the citizens of Paris rebelled against their government and held the city for two months. On the bloody suppression of this rebellion, Marx wrote one of his most famous pamphlets, *The Civil War in France*, an enthusiastic defence of the Commune.

Given the repeated failures and frustrations of worker's revolutions and movements, Marx also sought to understand capitalism, and spent a great deal of time in The British Library studying and reflecting on the works of political economists and economic data. By 1857 he had accumulated over 800 pages of notes and short essays on capital, landed property, wage labour, the state, foreign trade and the world market; this work however was not published until 1941, under the title *Grundrisse*. In 1859, Marx was able to publish *Contribution to the Critique of Political Economy*; his first serious economic work. In the early 1860s he worked on composing three large volumes, the *Theories of Surplus Value*, which discussed the theoreticians of political economy, particularly Adam Smith and David Ricardo. This work, that was published posthumously under the editorship of Karl Kautsky is often seen as the Fourth book of *Capital*, and constitutes one of the first comprehensive treatises on the history of economic thought. In 1867, well behind schedule, the first volume of *Capital* was published, a work which analyzed the capitalist process of production. Here, Marx elaborated his labour theory of value and his conception of surplus value and exploitation which he argued would ultimately lead to a falling rate of profit and the collapse of industrial capitalism. Volumes II and III remained mere manuscripts upon which Marx continued to work for the rest of his life and were published posthumously by Engels.

During the last decade of his life, Marx's health declined and he was incapable of the sustained effort that had characterized his previous work. He did manage to comment substantially on contemporary politics, particularly in Germany and Russia. His *Critique of the Gotha Programme*, opposed the tendency of his followers Wilhelm Liebknecht (1826-1900) and August Bebel (1840-1913) to compromise with the state socialism of Ferdinand Lassalle in the interests of a united socialist party. In his correspondence with Vera Zasulich, Marx contemplated the possibility of Russia's bypassing the capitalist stage of development and building communism on the basis of the common ownership of land characteristic of the village *Mir*.

3

Marxism

Marxism is the political philosophy and practice derived from the work of Karl Marx and Friedrich Engels. Any political practice or theory that is based on an interpretation of the works of Marx and Engels may be called Marxism. A theoretical presence of Marxist approaches in western academic fields of research is present in the disciplines of anthropology, media studies, theatre, history, sociological theory, economics, literary criticism, aesthetics and philosophy.

Overview

While there are many theoretical and practical differences among the various forms of Marxism, most forms of Marxism share these principles:

- an attention to the material conditions of people's lives and social relations among people
- a belief that people's consciousness of the conditions of their lives reflects these material conditions and relations
- an understanding of class in terms of differing relations of production and as a particular position within such relations

- an understanding of material conditions and social relations as historically malleable
- a view of history according to which class struggle, the evolving conflict between classes with opposing interests, structures each historical period and drives historical change
- a sympathy for the working class or proletariat
- and a belief that the ultimate interests of workers best match those of humanity in general

The main points of contention among Marxists are the degree to which they are committed to a workers' revolution as the means of achieving human emancipation and enlightenment, and the actual mechanism through which such a revolution might occur and succeed. Marxism is correctly but not exhaustively described as a variety of Socialism. Some Marxists, however, argue that no actual state has ever fully realized Marxist principles; other Marxists, such as Autonomists claim Marxist principles cannot be realized in any state construct seen through the 20th Century and would necessitate a re-conceptualization of the notion of state itself.

Classical Marxism

Classical Marxism refers to the body of theory directly expounded by Karl Marx and Friedrich Engels. The term "Classical Marxism" is often used to distinguish between "Marxism" as it is broadly understood and "what Marx believed," which is not necessarily the same thing. For example, shortly before he died in 1883, Marx wrote a letter to the French workers' leader Jules Guesde and to his own son-in-law Paul Lafargue, both of whom claimed to represent Marxist principles, in which he accused them of "revolutionary phrase-mongering" and of denying the value of reformist struggles. Paraphrasing Marx: "If that is Marxism, then I am not a Marxist." As the American Marx scholar Hal Draper remarked, "There are few thinkers in modern history, whose thought has been so badly misrepresented, by Marxists and anti-Marxists alike."

Marx and Engels

Karl Heinrich Marx (May 5, 1818, Trier, then part of Prussian Rhineland - March 14, 1883, London) was an immensely influential German philosopher, political economist, and socialist revolutionary. Marx addressed a wide variety of issues, including alienation and exploitation of the worker, the capitalist mode of production, and historical materialism. He is most famous, however, for his analysis of history in terms of class struggles, as summed up in the opening line of the introduction to the Communist Manifesto: "The history of all hitherto existing society is the history of class struggles." The influence of his ideas, already popular during his life, was greatly broadened by the victory of the Russian Bolsheviks in the October Revolution of 1917. Indeed, there are few parts of the world which were not significantly touched by Marxian ideas in the course of the 20th century.

Friedrich Engels (November 28, 1820, Wuppertal - August 5, 1895, London) was a 19th century German philosopher. He developed communist theory alongside Marx.

The two first met in person in September 1844. They discovered that they had similar views on philosophy and on capitalism and decided to work together, producing a number of works including *Die heilige Familie (The Holy Family)*. After the French authorities deported Marx from France in January 1845, Engels and Marx decided to move to Belgium, which then permitted greater freedom of expression than other countries in Europe. Engels and Marx returned to Brussels in January 1846, where they set up the Communist Correspondence Committee.

In 1847 Engels and Marx began writing a pamphlet together, based on Engels' '*The Principles of Communism.*' They completed the 12,000-word pamphlet in six weeks, writing it in such a manner as to make communism understandable to a wide audience, and published it as *The Communist Manifesto* in February 1848. In March, Belgium expelled both Engels and Marx. They moved to Cologne, where they began to publish a radical newspaper, the *Neue Rheinische Zeitung*. By 1849, both Engels and Marx had to leave Germany and moved to London. The Prussian authorities applied pressure on the British government to expel the two men, but Prime Minister Lord John Russell refused. With only the money that Engels could raise, the Marx family lived in extreme poverty.

After Marx's death in 1883, Engels devoted much of the rest of his life to editing and translating Marx's writings. He also contributed significantly to feminist theory and Marxist feminism in *Origins of the Family, Private Property, and the State*, conceiving, for instance, the concept of monogamous marriage as having arisen because of the domination of men over women. In this sense, he ties communist theory to the family, arguing that men have dominated women just as the capitalist class has dominated workers. Engels died in London in 1895.

4

Influences on Karl Marx

Influences on Karl Marx are commonly referred to as deriving from three sources: German idealist philosophy, French socialism, and English & Scottish political economy. Although this "three sources" model is an oversimplification, it still has some measure of truth.

German philosophy

Immanuel Kant

Immanuel Kant is believed to have had the greatest influence of any philosopher of modern times. Kantian philosophy was the basis on which the structure of Marxism was built - particularly as it was developed by Georg Hegel. Hegel's dialectical method, which was taken up by Karl Marx, was an extension of the method of reasoning by "antinomies" that Kant used.

Georg Hegel

Georg Hegel, by the time of his death, was the most prominent philosopher in Germany. His views were widely taught, and his students were highly regarded. His followers soon divided into right-wing and left-wing Hegelians. Theologically and politically the right-wing Hegelians offered a conservative interpretation of his work. They emphasized the compatibility between Hegel's philosophy and Christianity. Politically, they were orthodox. The left-wing Hegelians eventually moved to an atheistic position. In politics, many of them became revolutionaries. This historically important left-wing group included Ludwig Feuerbach, Bruno Bauer, Friedrich Engels, and Marx. They were often referred to as the Young Hegelians.

Marx's view of history, which came to be called historical materialism, is certainly influenced by Hegel's claim that reality (and history) should be viewed dialectically. Hegel believed that the direction of human history is characterized in the movement from the fragmentary toward the complete and the real (which was also a movement towards greater and greater rationality). Sometimes, Hegel explained, this progressive unfolding of the Absolute involves gradual, evolutionary accretion but at other times requires discontinuous, revolutionary leaps – episodic upheavals against the existing status quo. For example, Hegel strongly opposed slavery in the United States during his lifetime, and he envisioned a time when Christian nations would radically eliminate it from their civilization.

While Marx accepted this broad conception of history, Hegel was an idealist, and Marx sought to rewrite dialectics in materialist terms. He summarized the materialistic aspect of his theory of history in the 1859 preface to *A Contribution to the Critique of Political Economy*:

"In the social production of their existence, men inevitably enter into definite relations, which are independent of their will, namely relations of production appropriate to a given stage in the development

of their material forces of production. The totality of these relations of production constitutes the economic structure of society, the real foundation, on which arises a legal and political superstructure and to which correspond definite forms of social consciousness. The mode of production of material life conditions the general process of social, political and intellectual life. It is not the consciousness of men that determines their existence, but their social existence that determines their consciousness."

In this brief popularization of his ideas, Marx emphasized that social development sprang from the inherent contradictions within material life and the social superstructure. This notion is often understood as a simple historical narrative: primitive communism had developed into slave states. Slave states had developed into feudal societies. Those societies in turn became capitalist states, and those states would be overthrown by the self-conscious portion of their working-class, or proletariat, creating the conditions for socialism and, ultimately, a higher form of communism than that with which the whole process began. Marx illustrated his ideas most prominently by the development of capitalism from feudalism, and by the prediction of the development of socialism from capitalism.

Ludwig Feuerbach

Ludwig Feuerbach was a German philosopher and anthropologist. According to Feuerbach, social and political thought should take as their foundation people and their material needs. He held that an individual is the product of their environment, that the whole consciousness of a person is the result of the interaction of sensory organs and the external world. Marx (and Engels) saw in Feuerbach's emphasis on people and human needs a movement toward a materialistic interpretation of society.

In *The Essence of Christianity*, Feuerbach argued that God is really a creation of man and that the qualities people attribute to God are really qualities of humanity. Accordingly, Marx argued that it is the material world that is real and that our ideas of it are consequences, not causes, of the world. Thus, like Hegel and other philosophers, Marx distinguished between appearances and reality. However he did not believe that the material world hides from us the "real" world of the ideal; on the contrary, he thought that historically and socially specific ideology prevented people from seeing the material conditions of their lives clearly.

What distinguished Marx from Feuerbach was his view of Feuerbach's humanism as excessively abstract, and so no less a historical and idealist than what it purported to replace, namely the reified notion of God found in institutional Christianity that legitimized the repressive power of the Prussian state. Instead, Marx aspired to give ontological priority to what he called the "real life process" of real human beings, as he and Engels said in *The German Ideology* (1846):

"In direct contrast to German philosophy, which descends from heaven to earth, here we ascend from earth to heaven. That is to say, we do not set out from what men say, imagine, conceive, nor from men as narrated, thought of, imagined, conceived, in order to arrive at men in the flesh. We set out from real, active men, and on the basis of their real life process we demonstrate the development of the ideological reflexes and echoes of this life process. The phantoms formed in the human brain are also, necessarily, sublimates of their material life process, which is empirically verifiable and bound to material premises. Morality, religion, metaphysics, all the rest of ideology and their corresponding forms of consciousness, thus no longer retain the semblance of independence. They have no history, no development; but

men, developing their material production and their material intercourse, alter, along with this, their real existence, their thinking, and the products of their thinking. Life is not determined by consciousness, but consciousness by life."

Also, in his *Theses on Feuerbach* (1845), he writes that "the philosophers have only described the world, in various ways; the point is to change it." This opposition between, firstly, various subjective interpretations given by philosophers, which may be, in a sense, compared with *Weltanschauung* designed to legitimize the current state of affairs, and, secondly, the effective transformation of the world through *praxis*, which combines theory and practice in a materialist way, is what distinguishes "Marxist philosophers" from the rest of philosophers. Indeed, Marx's break with German Idealism involves a new definition of philosophy; Louis Althusser, founder of "Structural Marxism" in the 1960s, would define it as "class struggle in theory." Marx's movement away from university philosophy and towards the workers' movement is thus inextricably linked to his rupture with his earlier writings, which pushed Marxist commentators to speak of a "young Marx" and a "mature Marx," although the nature of this cut poses problems. A year before the Revolutions of 1848, Marx and Engels thus wrote *The Communist Manifesto*, which was prepared to an imminent revolution, and ended with the famous cry: "Proletarians of all countries, unite!." However, Marx's thought changed again following Louis-Napoleon Bonaparte's December 2, 1851 coup, which put an end to the French Second Republic and created the Second Empire which would last until the 1870 Franco-Prussian War. Marx thereby modified his theory of alienation exposed in the *Economic and Philosophical Manuscripts* of 1844 and would latter arrive to his theory of commodity fetishism, exposed in the first chapter of the first book of *Das Kapital* (1867). This abandonment of the early theory of alienation would be amply discussed, several Marxist theorists, including Marxist humanists such as the Praxis School, would return to it. Others, such as Althusser, would claim that the "epistemological break" between the "young Marx" and the "mature Marx" was such that no comparisons could be done between both works, marking a shift to a "scientific theory" of society.

The rupture with German Idealism and the Young Hegelians

Marx did not study directly with Hegel, but after Hegel died Marx studied under one of Hegel's pupils, Bruno Bauer, a leader of the circle of Young Hegelians to whom Marx attached himself. However, Marx and Engels came to disagree with Bruno Bauer and the rest of the Young Hegelians about socialism and also about the usage of Hegel's dialectic. From 1841, the young Marx progressively broke away from German idealism and the Young Hegelians. Along with Engels, who observed the Chartist movement in the United Kingdom, he cut away with the environment in which he grew up and encountered the proletariat in France and Germany.

He then wrote a scathing criticism of the Young Hegelians in two books, "The Holy Family" (1845), and *The German Ideology* (1845), in which he criticized not only Bauer but also Max Stirner's *The Ego and Its Own* (1844), considered as one of the founding book of individualist anarchism. Max Stirner claimed that all ideals were inherently alienating, and that replacing God by the Humanity, as did Ludwig Feuerbach in *The Essence of Christianity* (1841), was not sufficient. According to Stirner, any ideals, God, Humanity, the Nation, or even the Revolution alienated the "Ego".

Marx also criticized Proudhon, whom had become famous with his cry "Property is theft!," in *The Poverty of Philosophy* (1845).

Marx's early writings are thus a response towards Hegel, German Idealism and a break with the rest of the Young Hegelians. Marx, "stood Hegel on his head," in his own view of his role, by turning the idealistic dialectic into a materialistic one, in proposing that material circumstances shape ideas, instead of the other way around.

In this, Marx was following the lead of Feuerbach. His theory of alienation, developed in the *Economic and Philosophical Manuscripts* of 1844 (published in 1932), inspired itself from Feuerbach's critique of the alienation of Man in God through the objectivities of all his inherent characteristics (thus man projected on God all qualities which are in fact man's own quality which defines the "human nature.)" But Marx also criticized Feuerbach for being insufficiently materialistic, as Stirner himself had point out, and explained that the alienation described by the Young Hegelians was in fact the result of the structure of the economy itself. Furthermore, he criticized Feuerbach's conception of human nature in his sixth thesis on Feuerbach as an abstract "kind" which incarnated itself in each singular individual: "Feuerbach resolves the essence of religion into the essence of man (*menschliche Wesen*, human nature). But the essence of man is no abstraction inherent in each single individual. In reality, it is the ensemble of the social relations."

Thereupon, instead of founding itself on the singular, concrete individual subject, as did classic philosophy, including contractualism (Hobbes, Locke and Rousseau) but also political economy, Marx began with the totality of social relations: labour, language and all which constitute our human existence. He claimed that individualism was an essence the result of commodity fetishism or alienation. Although some critics have claimed that meant that Marx enforced a strict social determinism which destroyed the possibility of free will, Marx's philosophy in no way can be reduced to such determinism, as his own personal trajectory makes clear.

In 1844-5, when Marx was starting to settle his account with Hegel and the Young Hegelians in his writings, he critiqued the Young Hegelians for limiting the horizon of their critique to religion and not taking up the critique of the state and civil society as paramount. Indeed in 1844, by the look of Marx's writings in that period (most famous of which is the "Economic and Philosophical Manuscripts of 1844", a text that most explicitly elaborated his theory of alienation), Marx's thinking could have taken at least three possible courses: the study of law, religion, and the state; the study of natural philosophy; and the study of political economy. He chose the last as the predominant focus of his studies for the rest of his life, largely on account of his previous experience as the editor of the newspaper *Rheinische Zeitung* on whose pages he fought for freedom of expression against Prussian censorship and made a rather idealist, legal defence for the Moselle peasants' customary right of collecting wood in the forest (this right was at the point of being criminalized and privatized by the state). It was Marx's inability to penetrate beneath the legal and polemical surface of the latter issue to its materialist, economic, and social roots that prompted him to critically study political economy.

English and Scottish political economy

Political economy predates the 20th century division of the two disciplines of politics and economics, treating social relations and economic relations as interwoven. Marx built on and critiqued the most well-known political economists of his day, the British classical political economists.

Adam Smith and David Ricardo

From Adam Smith came the idea that the grounds of property is labour.

Marx critiqued Smith and Ricardo for not realizing that their economic concepts reflected specifically capitalist institutions, not innate natural properties of human society, and could not be applied unchanged to all societies. He proposed a systematic correlation between labour-values and money prices. He claimed that the source of profits under capitalism is value added by workers not paid out in wages. This mechanism operated through the distinction between "labour power", which workers freely exchanged for their wages, and "labour", over which asset-holding capitalists thereby gained control.

This practical and theoretical distinction was Marx's primary insight, and allowed him to develop the concept of "surplus value", which distinguished his works from that of Adam Smith and David Ricardo. Workers create enough value during a short period of the working day to pay their wages for that day (necessary labour); however, they continue to work for several more hours and continue to create value (surplus labour). This value is not returned to them but appropriated by the capitalists. Thus, it is not the capitalist ruling class that creates wealth, but the workers, the capitalists then appropriating this wealth to themselves. (Some of Marx's insights were seen in a rudimentary form by the "Ricardian socialist" school.) He developed this theory of exploitation in *Capital: A Critique of Political Economy*, a "dialectical" investigation into the forms value relations take.

Marx's theory of business cycles; of economic growth and development, especially in two sector models; and of the declining rate of profit, or crisis theory, are other important elements of Marx's political economy. Marx later made tentative movements towards econometric investigations of his ideas, but the necessary statistical techniques of national accounting only emerged in the following century. In any case, it has proved difficult to adapt Marx's economic concepts, which refer to social relations, to measurable aggregated stocks and flows. In recent decades, however, a loose "quantitative" school of Marxist economist has emerged. While it may be impossible to find exact measures of Marx's variables from price data, approximations of basic trends are possible.

French socialism

Jean-Jacques Rousseau

Rousseau was one of the first modern writers to seriously attack the institution of private property, and therefore is sometimes considered a forebear of modern socialism and communism, though Marx rarely mentions Rousseau in his writings. He argued that the goal of government should be to secure freedom, equality, and justice for all within the state, regardless of the will of the majority. From Jean-Jacques Rousseau came the idea of egalitarian democracy.

Charles Fourier and Henri de Saint-Simon

In 1833 France was experiencing a number of social problems arising out of the Industrial Revolution. A number of sweeping plans of reform were developed by thinkers on the left. Among the more grandiose were the plans of Charles Fourier and the followers of Saint-Simon. Fourier wanted to replace modern cities with utopian communities, while the Saint-Simonians advocated directing the economy by manipulating credit. Although these programs didn't have much support, they did expand the political and social imagination of their contemporaries, including Marx.

Louis Blanc

Louis Blanc is perhaps best known for originating the social principle, later adopted by Marx, of how labour and income should be distributed: "From each according to his abilities, to each according to his needs."

Pierre-Joseph Proudhon

Pierre-Joseph Proudhon participated in the February 1848 uprising and the composition of what he termed "the first republican proclamation" of the new republic. But he had misgivings about the new government because it was pursuing political reform at the expense of the socio-economic reform, which Proudhon considered basic. Proudhon published his own perspective for reform, *Solution du problème social*, in which he laid out a program of mutual financial cooperation among workers. He believed this would transfer control of economic relations from capitalists and financiers to workers. It was Proudhon's book '*What is Property?*' that convinced the young Karl Marx that private property should be abolished.

In one of his first works, *The Holy Family*, Marx said, "Not only does Proudhon write in the interest of the proletarians, he is himself a proletarian, an ouvrier. His work is a scientific manifesto of the French proletariat." Marx, however, disagreed with

Proudhon's anarchism and later published vicious criticisms of Proudhon. Marx wrote *The Poverty of Philosophy* as a refutation of Proudhon's *The Philosophy of Poverty*. In his socialism, Proudhon was followed by Mikhail Bakunin. After Bakunin's death, his libertarian socialism diverged into anarchist communism and collectivist anarchism, with notable proponents such as Peter Kropotkin and Joseph Déjacque.

Other influences

Engels

Marx's revision of Hegelianism was also influenced by Engels' book, "The Condition of the Working Class" in England in 1844, which led Marx to conceive of the historical dialectic in terms of class conflict and to see the modern working class as the most progressive force for revolution. Thereafter Engels and Marx worked together for the rest of Marx's life, so that the collected works of Marx and Engels are generally published together, almost as if the output of one person. Important publications, such as the *German Ideology* and the *Communist Manifesto*, were joint efforts. Engels says "I cannot deny that both before anid during my 40 years' collaboration with Marx I had a certain independent share in laying the foundation of the theory, and more particularly in its elaboration." But he adds :

"But the greater part of its leading basic principles, especially in the realm of economics and history, and, above all, their final trenchant formulation, belong to Marx. What I contributed - at any rate with the exception of my work in a few special fields - Marx could very well have done without me. What Marx accomplished I would not have achieved. Marx stood higher, saw further, and took a wider and quicker view than all the rest of us. Marx was a genius; we others were

at best talented. Without him the theory would not be by far what it is today. It therefore rightly bears his name."

(Frederick Engels, Ludwig Feuerbach and the End of Classical German Philosophy Part 4: Marx)

Antique materialism

Marx was influenced by Antique materialism, especially Epicurus (to whom Marx dedicated his thesis, "Difference of natural philosophy between Democritus and Epicurus," 1841) for his materialism and theory of clinamen which opened up a realm of liberty.

Lewis Morgan

Marx drew on Lewis H. Morgan and his social evolution theory. He wrote a collection of notebooks from his reading of Lewis Morgan but they are regarded as being quite obscure and only available in scholarly editions.

Giambattista Vico

Giambattista Vico propounded a cyclical theory of history, according to which human societies progress through a series of stages from barbarism to civilization and then return to barbarism. In the first stage (called the Age of the Gods) religion, the family, and other basic institutions emerge; in the succeeding Age of Heroes, the common people are kept in subjection by a dominant class of nobles; in the final stage (the Age of Men) the people rebel and win equality, but in the process society begins to disintegrate. The connection between Vico's theory of history and Marx's account of the evolution of society is apparent.

Charles Darwin

Marx read Darwin's *The Origin of Species* and recognized its value in supporting his theory of class struggle. He even sent Darwin a

Karl Marx

personally inscribed copy of *Das Kapital* in 1873. Marx understood that Darwin's work both helped to explain the internal struggles of human society, and provided a material explanation for the processes of nature.

In 1861, Karl Marx wrote to his friend Ferdinand Lassalle, "Darwin's work is most important and suits my purpose in that it provides a basis in natural science for the historical class struggle. Despite all shortcomings, it is here that, for the first time, 'teleology' in natural science is not only dealt a mortal blow but its rational meaning is empirically explained."

Having read Darwin's work and mentioned Darwin by name in *Das Kapital*, it is presumable that Marx may have been influenced to some degree by Darwin.

Exaggeration of Darwin's Influence

However, the depth of the influence, if any, would certainly seem to be greatly exaggerated by a number of religious fundamentalists who seek to paint Darwin's ideas as incredibly dangerous. There is no mention of Darwin or evolution in *The Communist Manifesto* -- not surprising, since Darwin's On the *Origin of Species* was published in 1859, 11 years later -- and the only reference to Darwin in *Das Kapital* amounts to short footnotes on technological specialization in manufacturing and industry.

Despite this, in *The Disasters Darwinism Brought to Humanity*, Harun Yahya (a Muslim creationist) writes: "Karl Marx, the founder of Communism, adapted Darwin's ideas, which deeply influenced him, to the dialectic process of history." Yahya also writes: "Marx revealed his sympathy for Darwin by dedicating his most important work, *Das Kapital*, to him."

This last bit is a common misconception that arose from a letter from Darwin to Edward Aveling, (who later became the lover of Marx's daughter, Eleanor). Aveling had written to Darwin about wanting to dedicate his book to him, but Darwin declined and Darwin's response became mixed with Karl Marx's papers when Eleanor Marx inherited her father's papers from Engels. The letter was published in 1931 in the Russian Communist magazine, *Under the Banner of Marxism*, which went on to suggest that the enclosures referred to in the letter might have been chapters from *Das Kapital* that dealt with evolution. It was not until 1975 that Aveling's letter to Darwin was discovered, debunking this myth.

Main ideas

The main ideas to come out of Marx and Engels' collective works include:

- **Exploitation**: Marx refers to the exploitation of an entire segment or class of society by another. He sees it as being an inherent feature and key element of capitalism and free markets. The profit gained by the capitalist is the difference between the value of the product made by the worker and the actual wage that the worker receives; in other words, capitalism functions on the basis of paying workers less than the full value of their labour, in order to enable the capitalist class to turn a profit. This profit is not however moderated in terms of risk vs. return.

- **Alienation**: Marx refers to the alienation of people from aspects of their "human nature" (*"Gattungswesen"*, usually translated as 'species-essence' or 'species-being).' He believes that alienation is a systematic result of capitalism. Under capitalism, the fruits of production belong to the employers, who expropriate the surplus created by others and in so doing generate alienated labour. Alienation describes objective features of a person's situation in capitalism - it isn't necessary for them to believe or feel that they are alienated.

- **Base and superstructure:** Marx and Engels use the "base-structure" metaphor to explain the idea that the totality of relations among people with regard to "the social production of their existence" forms the economic basis, on which arises a superstructure of political and legal institutions. To the base corresponds the social consciousness which includes religious, philosophical and other main ideas; the base conditions both the superstructure and the social consciousness. A conflict between the development of material productive forces and the relations of production causes social revolutions, and the resulting change in the economic basis will sooner or later lead to the transformation of the superstructure. For Marx, though, this relationship is not a one way process - it is reflexive; the base determines the superstructure in the first instance and remains the foundation of a form of social organization which then can act again upon both parts of the base-structure metaphor. The relationship between superstructure and base is considered to be a dialectical one, not a distinction between actual entities "in the world."

- **Class consciousness:** Class consciousness refers to the awareness, both of itself and of the social world around it, that a social class possess, and its capacity to act in its own rational interests based on this awareness. Thus class consciousness must be attained before the class may mount a successful revolution. Other methods of revolutionary action have been developed however, such as vanguardism.

- **Ideology**: Without offering a general definition for *ideology*, Marx on several instances has used the term to designate the production of images of social reality. According to Engels, "ideology is a process accomplished by the so-called thinker consciously; it is true, but with a false consciousness. The real motive forces impelling him remain unknown to him; otherwise it simply would not be an ideological process. Hence he imagines false or seeming motive forces." Because the ruling class controls the society's means of production, the superstructure of society, as well as its ruling ideas, will be determined according to what is in the ruling class's best interests. As Marx said famously in *The German Ideology*, "the ideas of the ruling class are in every epoch the ruling ideas, i.e. the class which is the ruling material force of society, is at the same time its ruling intellectual force." Therefore the ideology of a society is of enormous importance since it confuses the alienated groups and can create false consciousness such as commodity fetishism (perceiving labour as capital - a degradation of human life).

- **Historical materialism**: Historical materialism was first articulated by Marx, although he himself never used the term. It looks for the causes of developments and changes in human societies in the way in which humans collectively make the means to live, thus giving an emphasis, through economic analysis, to everything that co-exists with the economic base of society (e.g. social classes, political structures, ideologies.)

- **Political economy**: The term "political economy" originally meant the study of the conditions under which production was organized in the nation-states of the new-born capitalist system. Political economy, then, studies the mechanism of human activity in organizing material, and the mechanism of distributing the surplus or deficit that is the result of that activity. Political economy studies the means of production, specifically capital, and how this manifests itself in economic activity.

Class

Marx believed that the identity of a social class is derived from its relationship to the means of production (as opposed to the notion that class is determined by wealth alone, i.e., lower class, middle class, upper class.)

Marx describes several social classes in capitalist societies, including primarily:

- **The proletariat**: "those individuals who sell their labour power, (and therefore add value to the products), and who, in the capitalist mode of production, do not own the means of production." According to Marx, the capitalist mode of production establishes the conditions that enable the bourgeoisie to exploit the proletariat due to the fact that the worker's labour power generates a surplus value greater than the worker's wages.

- **The bourgeoisie**: those who "own the means of production" and buy labour power from the proletariat, thus exploiting the proletariat. The bourgeoisie may be further subdivided into the very wealthy bourgeoisie and the petit bourgeoisie.

- **The petit bourgeoisie** are those who employ labour, but may also work themselves. These may be small proprietors, land-holding peasants, or trade workers. Marx predicted that the petit bourgeoisie would eventually be destroyed by the constant reinvention of the means of production and the result of this would be the forced movement of the vast majority of the petit bourgeoisie to the proletariat.

Marx also identified various other classes such as:

- **The lumpenproletariat**: criminals, vagabonds, beggars, etc. People that have no stake in the economic system and will sell themselves to the highest bidder.

- **The landlords**: a class of people that were historically important, of which some still retain some of their wealth and power.

- **The peasantry and farmers**: this class he saw as disorganized and incapable of carrying out change. He also believed that this class would disappear, with most becoming proletariat but some becoming landowners.

Karl Marx

5

Marx's Theory of History

Historical materialism

Historical materialism is the methodological approach to the study of society, economics, and history which was first articulated by Karl Marx (1818-1883). Marx himself never used the term but referred to his approach as "the materialist conception of history." Historical materialism looks for the causes of developments and changes in the means of which human societies collectively make the means to live, thus giving an emphasis, through economic analysis, to everything that co-exists with the economic base of society (e.g. social classes, political structures, ideologies). The fundamental proposition of historical materialism is premised in the following materialist conception:

"It is not the consciousness of men that determines their existence, but their social existence that determines their consciousness."

-Karl Marx, Preface to A Contribution to the Critique of Political Economy Historical materialism as an explanatory system has been expanded and refined by thousands of academic studies since

Marx's death. Although Marx said he was only proposing a guideline to historical research, by the twentieth century the concept of historical materialism became a keystone of modern communist doctrine.

Key ideas

Historical materialism started from a fundamental underlying reality of human existence: that in order for human beings to survive and continue existence from generation to generation, it is necessary for them to produce and reproduce the material requirements of life. While this may seem obvious it was only with Marx that this was seen as foundation for understanding human society and historical development. Marx then extended this premise by asserting the importance of the fact that, in order to carry out production and exchange, people have to enter into very definite social relations, most fundamentally *production relations*.

However, production does not get carried out in the abstract, or by entering into arbitrary or random relations chosen at will. Human beings collectively work on nature but do not do the same work; there is a division of labour in which people not only do different jobs, but some people live from the work of others by owning the means of production. How this is accomplished depends on the type of society. Production is carried out through very definite relations between people. And, in turn, these production relations are determined by the level and character of the productive forces that are present at any given time in history. For Marx, productive forces refer to the means of production such as the tools, instruments, technology, land, raw materials, and human knowledge and abilities in terms of using these means of production.

Following Marx, writers who identify with historical materialism usually postulate that society has moved through a number of types or modes of production. That is, the character of the production relations is determined by the character of the productive forces; these could be the simple tools and instruments of early human existence, or the more developed machinery and technology of present age. The main modes of production Marx identified generally include primitive communism or tribal society (a prehistoric stage), ancient society, feudalism and capitalism. In each of these social stages, people interact with nature and produce their living in different ways. Any surplus from that production is allotted in different ways. Ancient society was based on a ruling class of slave owners and a class of slaves; feudalism based on landowners and serfs; and capitalism based on the capitalist class and the working class. The capitalist class privately owns the means of production, distribution and exchange (e.g. factories, mines, shops and banks) while the working class live by exchanging their socialized labour with the capital class for wages.

Marx identified the production relations of society (arising on the basis of given productive forces) as the economic base of society. He also explained that on the foundation of the economic base there arise certain political institutions, laws, customs, culture, etc., and ideas, ways of thinking, morality, etc. These constituted the political/ideological superstructure of society. That all of this not only have as their origin in the economic base but also ultimately correspond to the character and development of that economic base, i.e. the way people come together in order to produce and reproduce the material requirements of life.

Historical materialism can be seen to rest on the following principles:

1. The basis of human society is how humans work on nature to produce the means of subsistence.

2. There is a division of labour into social classes (relations of production) based on property ownership where some people live from the labour of others.

3. The system of class division is dependent on the mode of production.

4. The mode of production is based on the level of the productive forces.

5. Society moves from stage to stage when the dominant class is displaced by a new emerging class, by overthrowing the "political shell" that enforces the old relations of production no longer corresponding to the new productive forces. This takes place in the superstructure of society, the political arena in the form of revolution, whereby the underclass "liberates" the productive forces with new relations of production, and social relations, corresponding to it.

Marx's clearest formulation of his "Materialist Conception of History" was in the 1859 Preface to his book-*A contribution to the Critique of Political Economy*, whose relevant passage is reproduced here:

"In the social production of their existence, men inevitably enter into definite relations, which are independent of their will, namely relations of production appropriate to a given stage in the development of their material forces of production. The totality of these relations of production constitutes the economic structure of society, the real foundation, on which arises a legal and political superstructure and to which correspond definite forms of consciousness. The mode of production of material life conditions the general process of social, political and intellectual life. It is not the consciousness of men that determines their existence, but their social existence that determines their consciousness. At a certain stage of development, the material productive forces of society come into conflict with the existing relations of production or - this merely expresses the same thing in legal terms - with the property relations within the framework of which they have operated hitherto. From forms of development of the productive forces these relations turn into their fetters. Then begins an era of social revolution. The changes in the economic foundation lead sooner or later to the transformation of the whole immense superstructure. In studying such transformations it is always necessary to distinguish between the material transformation of the economic conditions of production, which can be determined with the precision of natural science, and the legal, political, religious, artistic or philosophic - in short, ideological forms in which men become conscious of this conflict and fight it out. Just as one does not judge an individual by what he thinks about himself, so one cannot judge such a period of transformation by its consciousness, but, on the contrary, this consciousness must be explained from the contradictions of material life, from the conflict existing between the social forces of production and the relations of production."

Perhaps the most influential recent defence of this passage and of relevant Marxian and Marxist assertions is G.A. Cohen's *Karl Marx's Theory of History: A Defence.*

Key implications in the study and understanding of History

Many writers note that historical materialism represented a revolution in human thought, and a break from previous ways of understanding the underlying basis of change within various human societies. The theory shows what Marx called "coherence" in human history, because of the fact that each generation inherits the productive forces developed previously and in turn further develops them before passing them on to the next generation. Further that this coherence increasingly involves more of humanity the more the productive forces develop and expand to bind people together in production and exchange.

This understanding counters the notion that human history is simply a series of accidents, either without any underlying cause or caused by supernatural beings or forces exerting their will on society. This posits that history is made as a result of struggle between different social classes rooted in the underlying economic base.

Marx's materialism

While the "historical" part of historical materialism does not cause a comprehension problem (i.e., it means the present is explained by analysing the past), the term materialism is more difficult. Historical materialism uses "materialism" to make three separate points, where the truth or falsehood of one point does not affect the others.

First there is metaphysical or philosophical materialism, in which matter-in-motion is primary and thought about matter-in-motion, or thought about abstractions, is secondary.

Second, there is belief that economic processes form the material base of society upon which institutions and ideas derive and rest. While the economy is the base structure of society, it does not follow that everything in history is determined by the economy, just as every feature of a house is not determined by its foundations.

Third, there is the idea that in the capitalist mode of production the behaviour of actors in the market economy (means of production, distribution and exchange, the relations of production) plays the major role in configuring society.

Historical materialism and the future

In his analysis of the movement of history, Marx predicted the breakdown of capitalism (as a result of class struggle and the falling rate of profit), and the establishment in time of a communist society in which class-based human conflict would be overcome. The means of production would be held in the common ownership and used for the common good.

Marxist beliefs about history

According to Marxist theorists, history develops in accordance with the following observations:

1. Social progress is driven by progress in the material, productive forces a society has at its disposal (technology, labour, capital goods, etc.)

2. Humans are inevitably involved in production relations (roughly speaking, economic relationships or institutions), which constitute our most decisive social relations.

3. Production relations progress, with a degree of inevitability, following and corresponding to the development of the productive forces.

4. Relations of production help determine the degree and types of the development of the forces of production. For example, capitalism tends to increase the rate at which the forces develop and stresses the accumulation of capital.

5. Both productive forces and production relations progress independently of mankind's strategic intentions or will.

6. The superstructure -- the cultural and institutional features of a society, its ideological materials -- is ultimately an expression of the mode of production (which combines both the forces and relations of production) on which the society is founded.

7. Every type of state is a powerful institution of the ruling class; the state is an instrument which one class uses to secure its rule and enforce its preferred production relations (and its exploitation) onto society.

8. State power is usually only transferred from one class to another by social and political upheaval.

9. When a given style of production relations no longer supports further progress in the productive forces, either further progress is strangled, or 'revolution' must occur.

10. The actual historical process is not predetermined but depends on the class struggle, especially the organization and consciousness of the working class.

This sketch is abstract - real historical understanding needed for developing political strategy and tactics must involve "concrete analysis of concrete conditions" (V.I. Lenin).

Alienation and freedom

Hunter-gatherer societies were structured so that the economic forces and the political forces were one and the same. The elements of force and relation operated together, harmoniously. In the feudal society, the political forces of the kings and nobility had their relations with the economic forces of the villages through serfdom. The serfs, although not free, were tied to both forces and, thus, not completely alienated. Capitalism, Marx argued, completely separates the economic and political forces, leaving them to have relations through a limiting government. He takes the state to be a sign of this separation - it exists to manage the massive conflicts of interest which arise between classes in all those societies based on property relations.

The history of historical materialism

Marx's attachment to materialism arose from his doctoral research on the philosophy of Epicurus, as well as his reading of Adam Smith and other writers in classical political economy. Historical materialism builds upon the idea that became current in philosophy from the sixteenth to eighteenth centuries that the development of human society has moved through a series of stages, from hunting and gathering, through pastoralism and cultivation, to commercial society.

Frederick Engels wrote: "I use 'historical materialism' to designate the view of the course of history, which seeks the ultimate causes and the great moving power of all important historic events in the economic development of society, in the changes in the modes of production and exchange, with the consequent division of society into distinct classes and the struggles of these classes."

Warnings against misuse

"One has to `leave philosophy aside,' one has to leap out of it and devote oneself like an ordinary man to the study of actuality, for which there exists also an enormous amount of literary material, unknown, of course, to the philosophers... Philosophy and the study of the actual world have the same relation to one another as masturbation and sexual love."

-Karl Marx and Friedrich Engels, The German Ideology

Marx himself took care to indicate that he was only proposing a guideline to historical research (*Leitfaden or Auffassung*), and was not providing any substantive "theory of history" or "grand philosophy of history," let alone a "master-key to history." Numerous times, he and Engels expressed irritation with dilettante academics who sought to knock up their skimpy historical knowledge as quickly as possible into some grand theoretical system that would explain "everything" about history. To their great annoyance, the materialist outlook was used as an excuse for not studying history.

In the 1872 Preface to the French edition of *Das Kapital* Vol. 1, Marx also emphasised that "There is no royal road to science, and only those who do not dread the fatiguing climb of its steep paths have a chance of gaining its luminous summits." Reaching a scientific understanding was hard work. Conscientious, painstaking research was required, instead of philosophical speculation and unwarranted, sweeping generalisations.

But having abandoned abstract philosophical speculation in his youth, Marx himself showed great reluctance during the rest of his life about offering any generalities or universal truths about human existence or human history. The first explicit and systematic summary of the materialist interpretation of history published, *Anti-Dühring*, was written by Frederick Engels.

One of the aims of Engels's polemic *Herr Eugen Dühring's Revolution in Science* (written with Marx's approval) was to ridicule the easy "world schematism" of philosophers, who invented the latest wisdom from behind their writing desks. Towards the end of his life, in 1877, Marx wrote a letter to editor of the Russian paper *Otetchestvennye Zapisky*, which significantly contained the following disclaimer:

"(...) If Russia is tending to become a capitalist nation after the example of the Western European countries, and during the last years she has been taking a lot of trouble in this direction - she will not succeed without having first transformed a good part of her peasants into proletarians; and after that, once taken to the bosom of the capitalist regime, she will experience its pitiless laws like other profane peoples. That is all. But that is not enough for my critic. He feels himself obliged to metamorphose my historical sketch of the genesis of capitalism in Western Europe into an historico-philosophic theory of the marche generale imposed by fate upon every people, whatever the historic circumstances in which it finds itself, in order that it may ultimately arrive at the form of economy which will ensure, together with the greatest expansion of the productive powers of social labour, the most complete development of man. But I beg his pardon. (He is both honouring and shaming me too much.)"

Marx goes on to illustrate how the same factors can in different historical contexts produce very different results, so that quick and easy generalisations are not really possible. To indicate how seriously Marx took research, it is interesting to note that when he died, his estate contained several cubic meters of Russian statistical publications (it was, as the old Marx observed, in Russia that his ideas gained most influence).

But what is true is that insofar Marx and Engels regarded historical processes as law-governed processes, the possible future directions of historical development were to a great extent *limited* and *conditioned* by what happened before. Retrospectively, historical processes could be understood to have happened by *necessity* in certain ways and not others, and to some extent at least, the most likely variants of the future could be specified on the basis of careful study of the known facts.

Towards the end of his life, Engels commented several times about the abuse of historical materialism. In a letter to Conrad Schmidt dated August 5, 1890, he stated that "And if this man (i.e., Paul Barth) has not yet discovered that while the material mode of existence is the *primum agens* this does not preclude the ideological spheres from reacting upon it in their turn, though with a secondary effect, he cannot possibly have understood the subject he is writing about. (...) The materialist conception of history has a lot of [dangerous friends] nowadays, to whom it serves as an excuse for not studying history. Just as Marx used to say, commenting on the French "Marxists" of the late 70s: "All I know is that I am not a Marxist." (...) In general, the word "materialistic" serves many of the younger writers in Germany as a mere phrase with which anything and everything is labeled without further study, that is, they stick on this label and then consider the question disposed of. But our conception of history is above all a guide to study, not a lever for construction after the manner of the Hegelian. All history must be studied afresh; the conditions of existence of the different formations of society must be examined individually before the attempt is made to deduce them from the political, civil law, aesthetic, philosophic, religious, etc., views corresponding to them. Up to now but little has been done here because only a few people have got down to it seriously. In this field we can utilize heaps of help, it is immensely big, and anyone who will work seriously can achieve much and distinguish himself. But instead of this too many of the younger Germans simply make use of the phrase historical materialism (and everything can be turned into a phrase) only in order to get their own relatively scanty historical knowledge - for economic history is still in its swaddling clothes! - constructed into a neat system as quickly as possible, and they then

Karl Marx

deem themselves something very tremendous. And after that a Barth can come along and attack the thing itself, which in his circle has indeed been degraded to a mere phrase."

Finally, in a letter to Franz Mehring, Frederick Engels dated 14 July 1893, Engels stated:

"...there is only one other point lacking, which, however, Marx and I always failed to stress enough in our writings and in regard to which we are all equally guilty. That is to say, we all laid, and were bound to lay, the main emphasis, in the first place, on the derivation of political, juridical and other ideological notions, and of actions arising through the medium of these notions, from basic economic facts. But in so doing we neglected the formal side - the ways and means by which these notions, etc., come about - for the sake of the content. This has given our adversaries a welcome opportunity for misunderstandings, of which Paul Barth is a striking example."

Historical materialism in Marxist thought

In 1880, about three years before Marx died; Friedrich Engels indicated that he accepted the usage of the term "historical materialism." Recalling the early days of the new interpretation of history, he stated:

"We, at that time, were all materialists, or, at least, very advanced free-thinkers, and to us it appeared inconceivable that almost all educated people in England should believe in all sorts of impossible miracles, and that even geologists like Buckland and Mantell should contort the facts of their science so as not to clash too much with the myths of the book of Genesis; while, in order to find people who dared to use their own intellectual faculties with regard to religious matters, you had to go amongst the uneducated, the "great unwashed," as they were then called, the working people, especially the Owenite Socialists." (Preface to the English edition of his pamphlet *Socialism: Utopian and Scientific*)

In a foreword to his essay *Ludwig Feuerbach and the End of Classical German Philosophy* (1886), three years after Marx's death, Engels claimed confidently that "In the meantime, the Marxist world outlook has found representatives far beyond the boundaries of Germany and Europe and in all the literary languages of the world."

In his old age, Engels speculated about a new cosmology or ontology which would show the principles of dialectics to be universal features of reality. He also drafted an article on *The part played by labour in the transition from Ape to Man*, apparently a theory of anthropogenesis which would integrate the insights of Marx and Charles Darwin(This is discussed by Charles Woolfson in *The Labour Theory of Culture: a Re-examination of Engels Theory of Human Origins*).

At the very least, Marxism had now been born, and "historical materialism" had become a distinct philosophical doctrine, subsequently elaborated and systematised by intellectuals like Eduard Bernstein, Karl Kautsky, Georgi Plekhanov and Nikolai Bukharin. Even so, up to the 1930s many of Marx's earlier works were still unknown, and in reality most self-styled Marxists had not read beyond Capital Vol. 1. Isaac Deutscher provides an anecdote about the knowledge of Marx in that era:

"*Capital* is a tough nut to crack, opined Ignacy Daszynski, one of the best known socialist "people's tribunes" around the turn of the 20th century, but anyhow he had not read it. But, he said, Karl Kautsky had read it, and written a popular summary of the first volume. He hadn't read this either, but Kazimierz Kelles-Krauz, the party theoretician, had read Kautsky's pamphlet and summarised it. He also had not read Kelles-Krauz's text, but the financial expert of the party, Hermann Diamand, had read it and had told him, i.e. Daszynski, everything about it."

After Lenin's death in 1924, Marxism was transformed into Marxism-Leninism and from there to Maoism or Marxism-Leninism-Mao Zedong Thought in China which some regard as the "true doctrine" and others as a "state religion."

In the early years of the 20th century, historical materialism was often treated by socialist writers as interchangeable with dialectical materialism, a formulation never used by Friedrich Engels however. According to many Marxists influenced by Soviet Marxism, historical materialism is a specifically sociological method, while dialectical materialism refers to a more general, abstract, philosophy. The Soviet orthodox Marxist tradition, influential for half a century, based itself on Joseph Stalin's pamphlet *Dialectical and Historical materialism* and on textbooks issued by the "Institute of Marxism-Leninism of the Central Committee of the Communist Party of the Soviet Union."

Recent versions of historical materialism

Several scholars have argued that historical materialism ought to be revised in the light of modern scientific knowledge. Jürgen Habermas believes historical materialism "needs revision in many respects," especially because it has ignored the significance of communicative action. Leszek Nowak argues explicitly for a post-Marxist historical materialism.

Göran Therborn has argued that the method of historical materialism should be applied to historical materialism as intellectual tradition, and to the history of Marxism itself.

In the early 1980s Paul Hirst and Barry Hindess elabourated a structural Marxism interpretation of historical materialism. Regulation theory, especially in the work of Michel Aglietta draws extensively on historical materialism.

Brill publishers of Leyden publish a journal called *Historical Materialism* which explores different strands of theory in the tradition of Marx, Engels and the Western Marxists.

Criticisms

Philosopher of science Karl Popper, in his Conjectures and Refutations, critiqued such claims of the explanatory power or valid application of historical materialism by arguing that it could explain or explain away any fact brought before it, making it unfalsifiable.

Underlying the dispute among historians are the different assumptions made about the definition or concept of "history" and "historiography." Different historians take a different view of what it is all about, and what the possibilities of historical and social scientific knowledge are.

Historians also differ greatly about questions such as (1) the kinds of generalisations which can be validly made about history, (2) about the kinds of causal connections which can validly be postulated in history, and (3) about the validity of different kinds of explanation of historical development.

Broadly, the importance of the study of history lies in the ability of history to explain the present. Historical Materialism is important in explaining history from a scientific perspective, by following the scientific method, as opposed to belief-system theories like Creationism and Intelligent Design which explain the present from a belief-system point of view.

It has been argued that the theoretical framework of Socio-biology explains certain facts better, than does Historical Materialism.

6

Marxist Schools of Thought

Marxism-Leninism

Marxism-Leninism is a communist ideological stream that emerged as the mainstream tendency amongst the Communist parties in the 1920s as it was adopted as the ideological foundation of the Communist International during Stalin's era.

However, in various contexts, different (and sometimes opposing) political groups have used the term "Marxism-Leninism" to describe the ideology that they claimed to be upholding.

History of the term

Within 5 years of Lenin's death, Joseph Stalin completed his rise to power in the Soviet Union. According to G. Lisichkin, Marxism-Leninism as a separate ideology was compiled by Stalin basically in his "The questions of Leninism" book. During the period of Stalin's rule in the Soviet Union, Marxism-Leninism was proclaimed the official ideology of the state.

Whether Stalin's practices actually followed the principles of Marx and Lenin is still a subject of debate amongst historians and political scientists. Trotskyists in particular believe that Stalinism contradicted authentic Marxism and Leninism, and they initially used the term "Bolshevik-Leninism" to describe their own ideology of anti-Stalinist (and later anti-Maoist) communism. Left communists rejected "Marxism-Leninism" as an anti-Marxist current.

The term *Marxism-Leninism* is most often used by those who believe that Lenin's legacy was successfully carried forward by Joseph Stalin (Stalinists). However, it is also used by some who repudiate Stalin, such as the supporters of Nikita Khrushchev.

After the Sino-Soviet split, communist parties of the Soviet Union and the People's Republic of China each claimed to be the sole intellectual heir to Marxism-Leninism. In China, they claim that Mao had "adapted Marxism-Leninism to Chinese conditions" evolved into the idea that he had updated it in a fundamental way applying to the world as a whole; consequently, the term "Marxism-Leninism-Mao Zedong Thought" (commonly known as Maoism) was increasingly used to describe the official Chinese state ideology as well as the ideological basis of parties around the world who sympathized with the Communist Party of China. Following the death of Mao, Peruvian Maoists associated with the Communist Party of Peru (Sendero Luminoso) subsequently coined the term Marxism-Leninism-Maoism, arguing that Maoism was a more advanced stage of Marxism.

Following the Sino-Albanian split, a small portion of Marxist-Leninists began to downplay or repudiate the role of Mao Zedong in the International Communist Movement in favour of the Party of Labour of Albania and a stricter adherence to Stalin.

In North Korea, Marxism-Leninism was officially superseded in 1977 by Juche, in which concepts of class and class struggle, in other words Marxism itself, play no significant role. However, the government is still sometimes referred to as Marxist-Leninist - or, more commonly, Stalinist - due to its political and economic structure (see History of North Korea).

In the other three "communist states" existing today - Cuba, Vietnam, and Laos - the ruling Parties hold Marxism-Leninism as their official ideology, although they give it different interpretations in terms of practical policy.

Current usage

Some contemporary communist parties continue to regard Marxism-Leninism as their basic ideology, although some have modified it to adapt to new and local political circumstances.

In party names, the appellation 'Marxist-Leninist' is normally used by a communist party who wishes to distinguish itself from some other (and presumably 'revisionist') communist party in the same country.

Popular confusion abounds concerning the complex terminology describing the various schools of Marxist-derived thought. The appellation 'Marxist-Leninist' is often used by those not familiar with communist ideology in any detail (e.g. many newspapers and other media) as a synonym for any kind of Marxism.

Post-Stalin Moscow-aligned communism

At the 22nd Congress of the Communist Party of the Soviet Union, Khrushchev made several ideological ruptures with his predecessor, Joseph Stalin. First, Khrushchev denounced the so-called Cult of Personality that had developed around Stalin, which ironically enough Khrushchev had a pivotal role in fostering decades earlier. More importantly, however, Khrushchev rejected the heretofore orthodox Marxist-Leninist tenet that class struggle continues even under socialism, which is ostensibly an intermediate stage between capitalism and communism. Rather, the State ought to rule in the name of all classes. A related principle that flowed from the former was the notion of peaceful co-existence, or that the newly-emergent socialist bloc could peacefully compete with the capitalist world, solely by developing the productive forces of society.

Euro communism

Beginning around the 1970s, various communist parties in Western Europe, such as the Partito Communista Italia in Italy and the Partido Communista España under Santiago Carillo tried to hew to a more independent line from Moscow. Particularly in Italy, they leaned on the theories of Antonio Gramsci, despite the fact that Gramsci happened to consider himself an orthodox Marxist-Leninist. This trend went by the name Euro communism.

Anti-revisionism

There are many proponents of Marxist-Leninism who rejected the theses of Khrushchev, particularly Marxists of the Third World. They believed that Khrushchev was unacceptably altering or "revising" the fundamental tenets of Marxism-Leninism, a stance from which the label "anti-revisionist" is derived. Typically, anti-revisionists refer to themselves simply as Marxist-Leninists, although they may be referred to externally by the following epithets.

Maoism

Maoism takes its name from Mao Zedong, the erstwhile leader of the Peoples Republic of China; it is the variety of anti-revisionism that took inspiration, and in some cases received material support, from China, especially during the Mao period. There are several key concepts that were developed by Mao. First, Mao concurred with Stalin that not only does class struggle continue under the dictatorship of the proletariat, it actually accelerates as long as gains are being made by the proletariat at the expense of the disenfranchised bourgeoisie. Second, Mao developed a strategy for revolution called Prolonged People's War in what he termed the semi-feudal countries of the Third World. Prolonged People's War relied heavily on the peasantry. Third, Mao wrote many theoretical articles on epistemology and dialectics, which he called contradictions.

Hoxhaism

Hoxhaism, so named because the central contribution of Albanian statesman Enver Hoxha, was closely aligned with China for a number of years, but grew critical of Maoism because of the so-called Three Worlds Theory put forth by elements within the Communist Party of China and because it viewed the actions of Chinese leader Deng Xiaoping unfavourably. Ultimately, however, Hoxhaism as a trend came to the understanding that Socialism had never existed in China at all.

7

Trotskyism

Trotskyism is the theory of Marxism as advocated by Leon Trotsky. Trotsky considered himself an orthodox Marxist and Bolshevik-Leninist, arguing for the establishment of a vanguard party. His politics differed sharply from those of Stalinism, most importantly in declaring the need for an international proletarian revolution (rather than socialism in one country) and unwavering support for a true dictatorship of the proletariat based on democratic principles.

Trotsky was, together with Lenin, the most important and well-known leader of the Russian Revolution and the international Communist movement in 1917 and the following years. Nowadays, numerous groups around the world continue to describe themselves as Trotskyist, although they have developed Trotsky's ideas in different ways. A follower of Trotskyist ideas is usually called a "Trotskyist" or (in an informal or pejorative way) a "Trotskyite" or "Trot."

Definition

James P. Cannon in his 1942 book *History of American Trotskyism* wrote that "Trotskyism is not a new movement, a new doctrine, but the restoration, the revival of genuine Marxism as it was expounded and practiced in the Russian revolution and in the early days of the Communist International." However, Trotskyism can be distinguished from other Marxist theories by four key elements.

- Support for the strategy of permanent revolution, in opposition to the Two Stage Theory of his opponents;
- Criticism of the post-1924 leadership of the Soviet Union, analysis of its features and after 1933, support for political revolution in the Soviet Union and in what Trotskyists term the deformed workers' states;
- Support for social revolution in the advanced capitalist countries through working class mass action;
- Support for proletarian internationalism.

On the political spectrum of Marxism, Trotskyists are considered to be on the left. They supported democratic rights in the USSR, opposed political deals with the imperialist powers, and advocated a spreading of the revolution throughout Europe and the East.

Origins of Trotskyism and the 1905 Russian Revolution

According to Trotsky, the term 'Trotskyism' was coined by Pavel Milyukov, (sometimes transliterated as 'Paul Miliukoff'), the ideological leader of the Constitutional Democratic party (Kadets) in Russia. Milyukov waged a bitter war against 'Trotskyism' "as early as 1905," Trotsky argues.

Trotsky was elected chairman of the St. Petersburg Soviet during the 1905 Russian Revolution. He pursued a policy of proletarian revolution at a time when other socialist trends advocated a transition to a "bourgeois" (capitalist) regime to replace the essentially feudal Romanov state. It was during this year that Trotsky developed the theory of Permanent Revolution, as it later became known (see below). In 1905, Trotsky quotes from a postscript to a book by Milyukov, *The elections to the second state Duma*, published no later than May 1907:

Those who reproach the Kadets with failure to protest at that time, by organising meetings, against the 'revolutionary illusions' of Trotskyism and the relapse into Blanquism, simply do not understand... the mood of the democratic public at meetings during that period." - *The elections to the second state Duma* by Pavel Milyukov

Milyukov suggests that the mood of the "democratic public" was in support of Trotsky's policy of the overthrow of the Romanov regime alongside a workers' revolution to overthrow the capitalist owners of industry, support for strike action and the establishment of democratically elected workers' councils or "soviets."

Theory of Permanent Revolution

In 1905, Trotsky formulated a theory that became known as the Trotskyist theory of Permanent Revolution. It may be considered one of the defining characteristics of Trotskyism. Until 1905, Marxists had only shown how a revolution in a European capitalist society could lead to a socialist one. But this excluded countries such as Russia. Russia in 1905 was widely considered to have not yet established a capitalist society, but was instead largely feudal with a small, weak and almost powerless capitalist class.

The theory of Permanent Revolution addressed the question of how such feudal regimes were to be overthrown, and how socialism could be established given the lack of economic prerequisites. Trotsky argued that in Russia only the working class could overthrow feudalism and win the support of the peasantry, but that the working class would not stop there. It would seize the moment to go on to win its own revolution against the weak capitalist class, establishing a workers' state, and appeal to the working class in the advanced capitalist countries to come to its aid, so that socialism could develop in Russia and worldwide.

The capitalist or bourgeois-democratic revolution

Revolutions in Britain in the 17th Century and in France in 1789 abolished feudalism, establishing the basic requisites for the development of capitalism. But Trotsky argues that these revolutions would not be repeated in Russia. In *Results and Prospects*, written in 1906, in which Trotsky outlines his theory in detail, he argues: "History does not repeat itself. However much one may compare the Russian Revolution with the Great French Revolution, the former can never be transformed into a repetition of the latter." In the French Revolution of 1789, France experienced what Marxists called a "bourgeois-democratic revolution" - a regime was established where the "bourgeoisie," (the French term approximating to "capitalists"), overthrew feudalism. The bourgeoisie then moved towards establishing a regime of "democratic" parliamentary institutions. But while democratic rights were extended to the bourgeoisie they did not, however, generally extend to a universal franchise, let alone to the freedom for workers to organise unions or to go on strike, without a considerable struggle by the working class.

But, Trotsky argues, countries like Russia had no "enlightened, active" revolutionary bourgeoisie which could play the same role, and the working class constituted a very small minority. In fact, even by the time of the European revolutions of 1848, Trotsky argued, "the bourgeoisie was already unable to play a comparable role. It did not want and was not able to undertake the

Karl Marx

revolutionary liquidation of the social system that stood in its path to power."

Weakness of the capitalists

The theory of Permanent Revolution considers that in many countries which are thought to have not yet completed their bourgeois-democratic revolution, the capitalist class oppose the creation of any revolutionary situation, in the first instance because they fear stirring the working class into fighting for its own revolutionary aspirations against their exploitation by capitalism. In Russia the working class, although a small minority in a predominantly peasant based society, were organised in vast factories owned by the capitalist class, in large working class districts. During the Russian Revolution of 1905, the capitalist class found it necessary to ally with reactionary elements such as the essentially feudal landlords and ultimately the existing Czarist Russian state forces, in order to protect their ownership of their property, in the form of the factories, banks, and so forth, from expropriation by the revolutionary working class.

According to the theory of Permanent Revolution, therefore, in economically backward countries the capitalist class is weak and incapable of carrying through revolutionary change. They are linked to and rely on the feudal landowners in many ways. Trotsky further argues that since a majority of branches of industry in Russia were originated under the direct influence of government measures, sometimes even with the help of Government subsidies, the capitalist class was again tied to the ruling elite. In addition, the capitalist class was subservient to European capital.

The working class steps in

Instead, Trotsky argued, only the 'proletariat' or working class was capable of achieving the tasks of that 'bourgeois' revolution. In

1905, the working class in Russia, a generation brought together in vast factories from the relative isolation of peasant life, saw the result of its labour as a vast collective effort, and the only means of struggling against its oppression in terms of a collective effort also, forming workers councils (soviets), in the course of the revolution of that year. In 1906, Trotsky argued:

The factory system brings the proletariat to the foreground... The proletariat immediately found itself concentrated in tremendous masses, while between these masses and the autocracy there stood a capitalist bourgeoisie, very small in numbers, isolated from the 'people,' half-foreign, without historical traditions, and inspired only by the greed for gain. — Trotsky, *Results and Prospects*

The Putilov Factory, for instance, numbered 12,000 workers in 1900, and, according to Trotsky, 36,000 in July 1917. The theory of Permanent Revolution considers that the peasantry as a whole cannot take on this task, because it is dispersed in small holdings throughout the country, and forms a heterogeneous grouping, including the rich peasants who employ rural workers and aspire to landlordism as well as the poor peasants who aspire to own more land. Trotsky argues: "All historical experience... shows that the peasantry are absolutely incapable of taking up an independent political role."

Trotskyists differ on the extent to which this is true today, but even the most orthodox tend to recognise in the late twentieth century a new development in the revolts of the rural poor, the self-organising struggles of the landless, and many other struggles which in some ways reflect the militant united organised struggles of the working class, and which to various degrees do not bear the marks of class divisions typical of the heroic peasant struggles of previous epochs. However, orthodox Trotskyists today still argue that the town and city based working class struggle is central to the task of a successful socialist revolution, linked to these struggles of the rural poor. They argue that the working class learns of necessity to conduct a collective struggle, for instance in trade unions, arising from its social conditions in the factories and workplaces, and that the collective consciousness it achieves as a result is an essential ingredient of the socialist reconstruction of society.

Although only a small minority in Russian society, the proletariat would lead a revolution to emancipate the peasantry and thus "secure the support of the peasantry" as part of that revolution, on whose support it will rely. But the working class, in order to improve their own conditions, will find it necessary to create a revolution of their own, which would accomplish both the bourgeois revolution and then establish a workers' state.

International revolution

Yet, according to classical Marxism, revolution in peasant based countries, such as Russia, prepares the ground ultimately only for a development of capitalism since the liberated peasants become small owners, producers and traders which leads to the growth of commodity markets, from which a new capitalist class emerges. Only fully developed capitalist conditions prepare the basis for socialism.

Trotsky agreed that a new socialist state and economy in a country like Russia would not be able to hold out against the pressures of a hostile capitalist world, as well as the internal pressures of its backward economy. The revolution, Trotsky argued, must quickly spread to capitalist countries, bringing about a socialist revolution which must spread world-wide. But this position was shared by all Marxists until 1924 when Stalin began to put forward the slogan of "Socialism in one country."

In this way the revolution is "permanent," moving of necessity first from the bourgeois revolution to the workers' revolution and from there uninterruptedly to European and world-wide revolutions. Socialism until then had always seen capitalism as an international enemy to be replaced internationally.

Origins of the term

An internationalist outlook of permanent revolution is found in the works of Karl Marx. The term "permanent revolution" is taken from a remark of Marx from his March 1850 Address: "it is our task," Marx said:

> To make the revolution permanent until all the more or less propertied classes have been driven from their ruling positions, until the proletariat has conquered state power and until the association of the proletarians has progressed sufficiently far - not only in one country but in all the leading countries of the world - that competition between the proletarians of these countries ceases and at least the decisive forces of production are concentrated in the hands of the workers.

> *- Marx, Address of the Central Committee to the Communist League*

Trotskyism and the 1917 Russian Revolution

During his leadership of the Russian revolution of 1905, Trotsky argued that once it became clear that the Tsar's army would not come out in support of the workers, it was necessary to retreat before the armed might of the state in as good an order as possible. In 1917, Trotsky was again elected chairman of the Petrograd soviet, but this time soon came to lead the Military Revolutionary Committee which had the allegiance of the Petrograd garrison, and carried through the October 1917 insurrection. Stalin wrote:

All practical work in connection with the organization of the uprising was done under the immediate direction of Comrade Trotsky, the President of the Petrograd Soviet. It can be stated with certainty that the Party is indebted primarily and principally to Comrade Trotsky for the rapid going over of the garrison to the side of the Soviet and the efficient manner in which the work of the Military Revolutionary Committee was organized.

- Stalin, *Pravda*, November 6, 1918

As a result of his role in the Russian Revolution of 1917, the theory of Permanent Revolution was embraced by the young Soviet state until 1924.

The Russian revolution of 1917 was marked by two revolutions: the relatively spontaneous February 1917 revolution, and the 25 October 1917 seizure of power by the Bolsheviks, who had won the leadership of the Petrograd soviet.

Before the February 1917 Russian revolution, Lenin had formulated a slogan calling for the 'democratic dictatorship of the proletariat and the peasantry,' but after the February revolution, through his April theses, Lenin instead called for "all power to the Soviets." Lenin nevertheless continued to emphasise however (as did Trotsky also) the classical Marxist position that the peasantry formed a basis for the development of capitalism, not socialism.

But also before February 1917, Trotsky had not accepted the importance of a Bolshevik style organisation. Once the February 1917 Russian revolution had broken out Trotsky admitted the importance of a Bolshevik organisation, and joined the Bolsheviks in July 1917. Despite the fact that many, like Stalin, saw Trotsky's role in the October 1917 Russian revolution as central, Trotsky says that without Lenin and the Bolshevik party the October revolution of 1917 would not have taken place.

As a result, since 1917, Trotskyism as a political theory is fully committed to a Leninist style of democratic centralist party organisation, which Trotskyists argue must not be confused with the party organisation as it later developed under Stalin. Trotsky had previously suggested that Lenin's method of organisation would lead to a dictatorship, but it is important to emphasise that after 1917 orthodox Trotskyists argue that the loss of democracy in the Soviet Union was caused by the failure of the revolution to successfully spread internationally and the consequent wars, isolation and imperialist intervention, not the Bolshevik style of organisation.

Lenin's outlook had always been that the Russian revolution would need to stimulate a Socialist revolution in Western Europe in order that this European socialist society would then come to the aid of the Russian revolution and enable Russia to advance towards socialism. Lenin stated:

We have stressed in a good many written works, in all our public utterances, and in all our statements in the press that... the socialist revolution can triumph only on two conditions. First, if it is given timely support by a socialist revolution in one or several advanced countries.

- Lenin, *Speech at Tenth Congress of the RCP(B)*

This outlook matched precisely Trotsky's theory of Permanent Revolution. Trotsky's Permanent Revolution had foreseen that the working class would not stop at the bourgeois democratic stage of the revolution, but proceed towards a workers' state, as happened in 1917. In 1917, Lenin changed his attitude to Trotsky's theory of Permanent Revolution and after the October revolution it was adopted by the Bolsheviks.

Lenin was met with initial disbelief in April 1917. Trotsky argues that:

Up to the outbreak of the February revolution and for a time after Trotskyism did not mean the idea that it was impossible to build a socialist society within the national boundaries of Russia (which "possibility" was never expressed by anybody up to 1924 and hardly came into anybody's head). Trotskyism meant the idea that the Russian proletariat might win the power in advance of the Western proletariat, and that in that case, it could not confine itself within the limits of a democratic dictatorship but would be compelled to undertake the initial socialist measures. It is not surprising, then, that the April theses of Lenin were condemned as Trotskyist. - Leon Trotsky, History of the Russian Revolution.

The 'legend of Trotskyism'

In *The Stalin School of Falsification*, Trotsky argues that what he calls the "legend of Trotskyism" was formulated by Zinoviev and Kamenev in collaboration with Stalin in 1924, in response to the criticisms Trotsky raised of Politburo policy. Orlando Figes argues that "The urge to silence Trotsky, and all criticism of the Politburo, was in itself a crucial factor in Stalin's rise to power."

During 1922-24, Lenin suffered a series of strokes and became increasingly incapacitated. Before his death in 1924, Lenin, while describing Trotsky as "distinguished not only by his exceptional abilities - personally he is, to be sure, the most able man in the present Central Committee," criticized him for "showing excessive preoccupation with the purely administrative side of the work" and "non-Bolshevism," and also requested that Stalin be removed from his position of General Secretary, but his notes remained suppressed until 1956. Zinoviev and Kamenev broke with Stalin in

1925 and joined Trotsky in 1926 in what was known as the United Opposition.

In 1926, Stalin allied with Bukharin who then led the campaign against "Trotskyism." In *The Stalin School of Falsification*, Trotsky quotes Bukharin's 1918 pamphlet, *From the Collapse of Czarism to the Fall of the Bourgeoisie*, which was reprinted by the party publishing house, 'Proletari,' in 1923.

In this pamphlet, Bukharin explains and embraces Trotsky's theory of permanent revolution, writing: "The Russian proletariat is confronted more sharply than ever before with the problem of the international revolution … The grand total of relationships which have arisen in Europe leads to this inevitable conclusion.

Thus, the *permanent revolution in Russia is passing into the European proletarian revolution.*" Yet it is common knowledge, Trotsky argues, that three years later, in 1926, "Bukharin was the chief and indeed the sole theoretician of the entire campaign against 'Trotskyism,' summed up in the struggle against the theory of the permanent revolution."

Trotsky wrote that the Left Opposition grew in influence throughout the 1920s, attempting to reform the Communist Party. But in 1927 Stalin declared "civil war" against them:

During the first ten years of its struggle, the Left Opposition did not abandon the program of ideological conquest of the party for that of conquest of power against the party. Its slogan was: reform, not revolution. The bureaucracy, however, even in those times, was ready for any revolution in order to defend itself against a democratic reform.

In 1927, when the struggle reached an especially bitter stage, Stalin declared at a session of the Central Committee, addressing himself to the Opposition: "Those cadres can be removed only by civil war!" What was a threat in Stalin's words became, thanks to a series of defeats of the European proletariat, a historic fact. The road of reform was turned into a road of revolution.

—Trotsky, Leon, *Revolution Betrayed*, p279, Pathfinder

Defeat of the European working class led to further isolation in Russia, and further suppression of the Opposition. Trotsky argued that the "so-called struggle against 'Trotskyism' grew out of the bureaucratic reaction against the October Revolution [of 1917]." He responded to the one sided civil war with his *Letter to the Bureau of Party History*, (1927), contrasting what he claimed to be the falsification of history with the official history of just a few years before. He further accused Stalin of derailing the Chinese revolution, and causing the massacre of the Chinese workers:

In the year 1918, Stalin, at the very outset of his campaign against me, found it necessary, as we have already learned, to write the following words:

"All the work of practical organization of the insurrection was carried out under the direct leadership of the Chairman of the Petrograd Soviet, comrade Trotsky..." (Stalin, Pravda, Nov. 6, 1918)

With full responsibility for my words, I am now compelled to say that the cruel massacre of the Chinese proletariat and the Chinese Revolution at its three most important turning points, the strengthening of the position of the trade union agents of British imperialism after the General Strike of 1926, and, finally, the general weakening of the position of the Communist International

and the Soviet Union, the party owes principally and above all to
Stalin.

—Trotsky, Leon, *The Stalin School of Falsification*, p87,
Pathfinder (1971)

Trotsky was sent into internal exile and his supporters were
jailed. Victor Serge, for instance, first "spent six weeks in a cell"
after a visit at midnight, then 85 days in an inner GPU cell, most of
it in solitary confinement. He details the jailing of the Left
Opposition. The Left Opposition, however, continued to work in
secret within the Soviet Union. Trotsky was eventually exiled to
Turkey. He moved from there to Norway, and finally to Mexico.

After 1928, the various Communist Parties throughout the
world expelled Trotskyists from their ranks. Most Trotskyists
defend the economic achievements of the planned economy in the
Soviet Union during the 1920s and 1930s, despite the
"misleadership" of the soviet bureaucracy, and what they claim to
be the loss of democracy. Trotskyists claim that in 1928 inner party
democracy, and indeed soviet democracy, which was at the
foundation of Bolshevism, had been destroyed within the various
Communist Parties. Anyone who disagreed with the party line was
labeled a Trotskyist and even a fascist.

In 1937, Stalin again unleashed a political terror against the
Left Opposition and many of the remaining 'Old Bolsheviks'
(those who had played key roles in the October Revolution in
1917), in the face of increased opposition, particularly in the army.

Degenerated workers' state

Trotsky developed the theory that the Russian workers' state had
become a "degenerated workers' state." Capitalist rule had not
been restored, and nationalized industry and economic planning,

instituted under Lenin, were still in effect. However, Trotskyists claim that the state was controlled by a bureaucratic caste with interests hostile to those of the working class. Stalinism was a counter-revolutionary force.

Trotsky defended the Soviet Union against attack from foreign powers and against internal counter-revolution, but called for a political revolution within the USSR to bring about his version of socialist democracy: "The bureaucracy can be removed only by a revolutionary force." He argued that if the working class did not take power away from the "Stalinist" bureaucracy, the bureaucracy would restore capitalism in order to enrich itself. In the view of many Trotskyists, this is exactly what has happened since the beginning of Glasnost and Perestroika in the USSR. Some argue that the adoption of market socialism by the People's Republic of China has also led to capitalist counter-revolution. Many of Trotsky's criticisms of Stalinism were described in his book, *The Revolution Betrayed*.

"Trotskyist" has been used by "Stalinists" to mean a traitor; in the Spanish Civil War, being called a "Trot," "Trotskyist" or "Trotskyite" by the USSR-supported elements implied that the person was some sort of fascist spy or agent provocateur. For instance, George Orwell, a prominent Anti-Stalinist writer, wrote about this practice in his book *Homage to Catalonia* and in his essay *Spilling the Spanish Beans*. In his book *Animal Farm*, an allegory for the Russian Revolution, he represented Trotsky with the character "Snowball" and Stalin with the character "Napoleon." Emmanuel Goldstein in Orwell's *Nineteen Eighty-Four* has also been linked to Trotsky.

In 1937 Trotsky wrote:

To maintain itself, Stalinism is now forced to conduct a direct civil war against Bolshevism, under the name of "Trotskyism," not only in the USSR but also in Spain. The old Bolshevik Party is dead, but Bolshevism is raising its head everywhere. To deduce Stalinism from Bolshevism or from Marxism is the same as to deduce, in a larger sense, counterrevolution from revolution.

—Trotsky, Leon, *Stalinism and Bolshevism* 1937, in *Living Marxism,* No. 18, April 1990.

Stalin put out a general call for the assassination of Trotsky, and he was finally killed with an ice axe in Mexico in 1940, by Ramon Mercader, a Spanish supporter of Stalin, under direct orders from the GPU.

Founding of the Fourth International

In 1938, Trotsky and the organisations that supported his outlook established the Fourth International. He said that only the Fourth International, basing itself on Lenin's theory of the vanguard party, could lead the world revolution, and that it would need to be built in opposition to both the capitalists and the Stalinists.

Trotsky argued that the defeat of the German working class and the coming to power of Hitler in 1933 was due in part to the mistakes of the Third Period policy of the Communist International and that the subsequent failure of the Communist Parties to draw the correct lessons from those defeats showed that they were no longer capable of reform, and a new international organisation of the working class must be organised.

At the time of the founding of the Fourth International in 1938 Trotskyism was a mass political current in Vietnam, Sri Lanka and slightly later Bolivia. There was also a substantial Trotskyist movement in China which included the founding father of the Chinese Communist movement, Chen Duxiu, amongst its number. Wherever Stalinists gained power, they made it a priority to hunt down Trotskyists and treated them as the worst of enemies.

The Fourth International suffered repression and disruption through the Second World War. Isolated from each other, and faced with political developments quite unlike those anticipated by Trotsky, some Trotskyist organizations decided that the USSR no longer could be called a degenerated workers state and withdrew from the Fourth International. After 1945 Trotskyism was smashed as a mass movement in Vietnam and marginalised in a number of other countries.

The International Secretariat of the Fourth International organised an international conference in 1946, and then World Congresses in 1948 and 1951 to assess the expropriation of the capitalists in Eastern Europe and Yugoslavia, the threat of a Third World War, and the tasks for revolutionaries. The Eastern European Communist-led governments which came into being after World War II without a social revolution were described by a resolution of the 1948 congress as presiding over capitalist economies. By 1951, the Congress had concluded that they had become "deformed workers' states." As the Cold War intensified, the FI's 1951 World Congress adopted theses by Michel Pablo that anticipated an international civil war. Pablo's followers considered that the Communist Parties, insofar as they were placed under pressure by the real workers' movement, could escape Stalin's manipulations and follow a revolutionary orientation.

The 1951 Congress argued that Trotskyists should start to conduct systematic work inside those Communist Parties which were followed by the majority of the working class. However, the

ISFI's view that the Soviet leadership was counter-revolutionary remained unchanged. The 1951 Congress argued that the Soviet Union took over these countries because of the military and political results of World War II, and instituted nationalized property relations only after its attempts at placating capitalism failed to protect those countries from the threat of incursion by the West.

Pablo began expelling large numbers of people who did not agree with his thesis and who did not want to dissolve their organizations within the Communist Parties. For instance, he expelled the majority of the French section and replaced its leadership. As a result, the opposition to Pablo eventually rose to the surface, with an open letter to Trotskyists of the world, by Socialist Workers Party leader James P. Cannon.

The Fourth International split in 1953 into two public factions. The International Committee of the Fourth International was established by several sections of the International as an alternative centre to the International Secretariat, in which they felt a revisionist faction led by Michel Pablo had taken power. From 1960, a number of ICFI sections started to reunify with the IS. After the 1963 reunification congress which established the reunified Fourth International, the French and British sections maintained the ICFI. Other groups took different paths and originated the present complex map of Trotskyist groupings.

Trotskyist movements

Latin America

Trotskyism has had some influence in some recent major social upheavals, particularly in Latin America. In particular, Venezuelan president Hugo Chavez declared himself to be a Trotskyist during his swearing in of his cabinet two days before his own inauguration on 10 January 2007.

The Bolivian Trotskyist party *(Partido Obrero Revolucionario,* POR) became a mass party in the period of the late 1940s and early 1950s, and together with other groups played a central role during and immediately after the period termed the Bolivian National Revolution.

In Brazil, as an officially recognised platform or faction of the PT, the Trotskyist Movimento Convergência Socialista (CS), now the United Socialist Workers' Party saw a number of its members elected to national, state and local legislative bodies during the 1980s. Today the Socialism and Freedom Party (PSOL) is described as Trotskyist. Its presidential candidate in the 2006 general elections, Heloísa Helena is termed a Trotskyist who was a member of the Workers Party of Brazil (PT), a legislative deputy in Alagoas and in 1999 was elected to the Federal Senate. Expelled from the PT in December 2003, she helped found PSOL, in which various Trotskyist groups play a prominent role.

During the 1980s in Argentina, the Trotskyist party founded in 1982 by Nahuel Moreno, MAS, (Movimiento al Socialismo, Movement toward Socialism), claimed to be the "largest Trotskyist party" in the world, before it broke into a number of different fragments in the late 1980s, including the present-day MST. During the 1980s, it obtained around 10% of the electorate, representing 3.5 million voters. Today the Workers' Party in Argentina has an electoral base in Salta Province in the far north, particularly in the city of Salta itself, and has become the third political force in the provinces of Tucuman, also in the north, and Santa Cruz, in the south.

Asia

In Indochina during the 1930s, Vietnamese Trotskyism led by Ta Thu Thau was a significant current, particularly in Saigon.

In Sri Lanka, the Lanka Sama Samaja Party (LSSP) expelled its pro-Moscow wing in 1940, becoming a Trotskyist-led party. In the general election of 1947 the LSSP became the main opposition party, winning 10 seats. It joined the Trotskyist Fourth International in 1950, and led a general strike (Hartal) in 1953.

Europe

In France, 10% of the electorate voted in 2002 for parties calling themselves Trotskyist.

In the UK in the 1980s, the entrist Militant tendency won three members of parliament and effective control of Liverpool City Council while in the Labour Party. Described as "Britain's fifth most important political party" in 1986 it played a prominent role in the 1989-1991 mass anti-poll tax movement which was widely thought to have led to the downfall of British Prime Minister Margaret Thatcher.

Trotskyism today

There is a wide range of Trotskyist organisations around the world. These include but are not limited to:

The reunified Fourth International

The reunified Fourth International derives from the 1963 reunification of the majorities of the two public factions into which the FI split in 1953: the International Secretariat of the Fourth International (ISFI) and the International Committee of the Fourth International (ICFI). It is often referred to as the United Secretariat of the Fourth International, the name of its leading committee before 2003. It is widely described as the largest contemporary Trotskyist organisation. Its best known section is the Ligue Communiste Revolutionnaire of France.

In many countries its sections work within working class parties, and alliances, in which Trotskyists are a minority.

Committee for a Workers' International

The Committee for a Workers' International (CWI) was founded in 1974 and now has sections in over 35 countries. Before 1997, most organisations affiliated to the CWI sought to build an entrist Marxist wing within the large social democratic parties. Since the early 1990s it has argued that most social democratic parties have moved so far to the right that there is little point trying to work within them. Instead the CWI has adopted a range of tactics, mostly seeking to build independent parties, but in some cases working within other broad working-class parties.

International Socialist Tendency

The International Socialist Tendency, led by the Socialist Workers Party, the largest Trotskyist group in Britain.

Internationalist Communist Union

In France, the LCR is rivaled by Lutte Ouvrière. That group is the French section of the Internationalist Communist Union (UCI). UCI has small sections in a handful of other countries. It focuses its activities, whether propaganda or intervention, within the industrial proletariat.

International Marxist Tendency

The Committee for a Marxist International (CMI) split from CWI, when CWI abandoned entryism. Since 2006, it has been known as the International Marxist Tendency (IMT). CMI/IMT groups continue the policy of entering mainstream social democratic, communist or radical parties. In Pakistan, the group had three MPs elected as candidates of the Pakistan Peoples Party. Leading figures in CMI/IMT are Ted Grant (who died in 2006) and Alan Woods.

International Committee of the Fourth International

There used to be several groups claiming the name of International Committee of the Fourth International, but now only two remain. Further, only one of these ICFIs has national groups in more than one country. Its sections are called Socialist Equality Parties and publish the World Socialist Web Site.

Others

The list of Trotskyist internationals shows that there are a large number of other multinational tendencies that stand in the tradition of Leon Trotsky. Some Trotskyist organisations are only organised in one country.

8

Western Marxism

Western Marxism is a term used to describe a wide variety of Marxist theoreticians based in Western and Central Europe (and more recently North America), in contrast with philosophy in the Soviet Union. While Georg Lukács's *History and Class Consciousness* and Karl Korsch's *Marxism and Philosophy*, first published in 1923, are often seen as the works which inaugurated this current, the phrase itself was coined much later by Maurice Merleau-Ponty. Its proponents have mostly (but not exclusively) been professional academics.

Distinctive elements

Although there have been many schools of Marxism, such as Austromarxism or the Left Communism of Antonie Pannekoek or Rosa Luxemburg, that are sharply distinguished from Marxism-Leninism, the term "Western Marxism" is usually applied to Marxist theorists who downplay the primacy of economic analysis, concerning themselves instead with abstract and philosophical areas of Marxism. In its earliest years, Western Marxism's most characteristic element was a stress on the Hegelian and humanist components of Marx's thought, but later forms of Western Marxism, such as Structural Marxism, have been just as strongly anti-humanist. Western Marxism often emphasises the importance of the study of culture for an adequate Marxist understanding of society. Western Marxists have thus elaborated often-complex variations on the theories of ideology and superstructure, which are only thinly sketched in the writings of Marx and Engels themselves.

Political commitments

Western Marxists have varied in terms of political commitment: Lukács, Gramsci and Althusser (famous for his supposed "anti-humanism") were all members of Soviet-aligned parties; Karl Korsch was heavily critical of Soviet Marxism, advocating council communism and later becoming increasingly interested in anarchism; the theorists of The Frankfurt School tended towards political quietism, although Herbert Marcuse became known as the 'father of the New Left;' Sartre, Merleau-Ponty and Lefebvre were, at different periods, supporters of the Communist Party of France, but all would later become disillusioned with it; Ernst Bloch lived in and supported the Soviet Union, but lost faith in it towards the end of his life. Maoism and Trotskyism also influenced Western Marxism.

Structural Marxism

Structural Marxism is an approach to Marxism based on structuralism, primarily associated with the work of the French theorist Louis Althusser and his students. It was influential in France during the late 1960s and 1970s, and also came to influence philosophers, political theorists and sociologists outside of France during the 1970s.

Neo-Marxism

Neo-Marxism is a loose term for various twentieth-century approaches that amend or extend Marxism and Marxist theory, usually by incorporating elements from other intellectual traditions (for example: critical theory, which incorporates psychoanalysis; Erik Olin Wright's theory of contradictory class locations, which incorporates Weberian sociology; and critical criminology, which incorporates anarchism. As with many uses of the prefix neo-, many theorists and groups designated "neo-Marxist" attempted to supplement the perceived deficiencies of orthodox Marxism or dialectical materialism.

One such approach might be Marxist humanism, a 20th century school that hearkened back to the early writings of Marx before the influence of Engels, which focused on dialectical idealism rather than dialectical materialism, and thus rejected the perceived economic determinism of the late Marx, focusing instead on a non-physical, psychological revolution. It was thus far more libertarians and related to strains of anarchism. It also put more of an emphasis on the evils of global capitalism. It was bound up with the student movements of the 1960s. Many prominent Neo-Marxists such as Herbert Marcuse were sociologists and psychologists.

Neo-Marxism comes under the broader heading of New Left thinking. Neo-Marxism is also used frequently to describe the opposition to inequalities experienced by Lesser Developed Countries in a globalized world. In a sociological sense, neo-Marxism adds Max Weber's broader understanding of social inequality, such as status and power, to Marxist philosophy.

Strains of neo-Marxism include: Hegelian-Marxism, Critical Theory, Analytical Marxism, and French Structural Marxism (closely related to structuralism).

The Frankfurt School

The Frankfurt School is a school of neo-Marxist critical theory, social research, and philosophy. The grouping emerged at the Institute for Social Research (*Institut für Sozialforschung*) of the University of Frankfurt am Main in Germany when Max Horkheimer became the Institute's director in 1930. The term "Frankfurt School" is an informal term used to designate the thinkers affiliated with the Institute for Social Research or who were influenced by it. It is not the title of any institution, and the main thinkers of the Frankfurt School did not use the term to describe themselves.

The Frankfurt School gathered together dissident Marxists, severe critics of capitalism who believed that some of Marx's followers had come to parrot a narrow selection of Marx's ideas, usually in defence of orthodox Communist or Social-Democratic parties. Influenced especially by the failure of working-class revolutions in Western Europe after World War I and by the rise of Nazism in an economically and technologically advanced nation (Germany), they took up the task of choosing what parts of Marx's thought might serve to clarify social conditions that Marx himself had never seen. They drew on other schools of thought to fill in Marx's perceived omissions. Max Weber exerted a major influence, as did Sigmund Freud (as in Herbert Marcuse's Freudo-Marxist synthesis in the 1954 work *Eros and Civilization*). Their emphasis on the "critical" component of theory was derived significantly from their attempt to overcome the limits of positivism, crude materialism, and phenomenology by returning to Kant's critical philosophy and its successors in German idealism, principally Hegel's philosophy, with its emphasis on negation and contradiction as inherent properties of reality. A key influence also came from the publication in the 1930s of Marx's *Economic-Philosophical Manuscripts* and *The German Ideology*, which showed the continuity with Hegelianism that underlay Marx's thought. Marcuse was one of the first to articulate the theoretical significance of these texts.

Critical theory

Critical theory, in sociology and philosophy, is shorthand for *critical theory of society*. It is a label used by the Frankfurt School, their intellectual and social network, and those influenced by them intellectually to describe their own work. The work of the School is oriented toward radical social change, in contradiction to "traditional theory," i.e. theory in the positivistic, scientistic, or purely observational mode. In literature and literary criticism and cultural studies, by contrast, "critical theory" means something quite different, namely theory used in criticism.

The original critical social theorists were Marxists, and there is some evidence that in their choice of the phrase "critical theory of society" they were in part influenced by its sounding less politically controversial than "Marxism." Nevertheless there were other substantive reasons for this choice. First, they were explicitly linking up with the critical philosophy of Immanuel Kant, where the term *critique* meant philosophical reflection on the limits of claims made for certain kinds of knowledge and a direct connection between such critique and the emphasis on moral autonomy. In an intellectual context defined by dogmatic positivism and scientism on the one hand and dogmatic "scientific socialism" on the other, critical theory meant to rehabilitate through its philosophically critical approach an orientation toward revolutionary agency, or at least its possibility, at a time when it seemed in decline.

Second, in the context of both Marxist-Leninist and Social-Democratic orthodoxy, which emphasized Marxism as a new kind of positive science, they were linking up with the implicit epistemology of Karl Marx's work, which presented itself as critique, as in Marx's "Capital: A Critique of Political Economy." That is, they emphasized that Marx was attempting to create a new kind of critical analysis oriented toward the unity of theory and revolutionary practice rather than a new kind of positive science. Critique in this Marxian sense meant taking the ideology of a society (e.g. "freedom of the individual" or "equality" under capitalism) and critiquing it by comparing it with the social reality of that very society (e.g. subordination of the individual to the class structure or real social inequality under capitalism). It also, especially in the Frankfurt School version, meant critiquing the existing social reality in terms of the potential for human freedom and happiness that existed within that same reality (e.g. using technologies for the exploitation of nature that could be used for the conservation of nature).

The First Phase

The intellectual influences on and theoretical focus of the first generation of Frankfurt School critical theorists can be summarized as follows:

The historical situation: Transition from small-scale entrepreneurial capitalism to monopoly capitalism and imperialism; socialist labour movement grows, turns reformist; emergence of warfare/welfare state; Russian revolution and rise of Communism; neotechnic period; emergence of mass media and mass culture, "modern" art; rise of Nazism.

Weberian theory: comparative historical analysis of Western rationalism in capitalism, the modern state, secular scientific rationality, culture, and religion; analysis of the forms of domination in general and of modern rational-legal bureaucratic domination in particular; articulation of the distinctive, hermeneutic method of the social sciences.

Freudian theory: critique of the repressive structure of the "reality principle" of advance civilization and of the normal neurosis of everyday life; discovery of the unconscious, primary-process thinking, and the impact of the Oedipus complex and of anxiety on psychic life; analysis of the psychic bases of authoritarianism and irrational social behaviour, psychic Thermidor.

Critique of Positivism: critique of positivism as philosophy, as scientific methodology, as political ideology, and as everyday conformism; rehabilitation of --- negative --- dialectic, return to Hegel; appropriation of critical elements in phenomenology, historicism, existentialism, critique of their ahistorical, idealist tendencies; critique of logical positivism and pragmatism.

Aesthetic modernism: critique of "false" and reified experience by breaking through its traditional forms and language; projection of alternative modes of existence and experience; liberation of the unconscious; consciousness of unique, modern situation; appropriation of Kafka, Proust, Schoenberg, Breton; critique of the culture industry and "affirmative" culture; aesthetic utopia.

Marxian theory: critique of bourgeois ideology; critique of alienated labour; historical materialism; history as class struggle and exploitation of labour in different bodes of production;

systems analysis of capitalism as extraction of surplus labour through free labour in the free market; unity of theory and practice; analysis for the sake of revolution, socialist democracy, classless society.

Culture theory: critique of mass culture as suppression and absorption of negation, as integration into status quo; critique of Western culture as culture of domination of external and internal nature; dialectic differentiation of emancipatory and repressive dimensions of elite culture; Nietzsche's transvaluation and Schiller's aesthetic education.

These influences combined to create the **Critical Theory of Culture (First Generation)**: Responding to the intensification of unfreedom and irrationality in industrial, advanced capitalist society---culminating in fascism---critical theory is a comprehensive, ideology-critical, historically self-reflective, body of theory aiming simultaneously to explain and combat domination and alienation and help bring about a rational, humane, democratic, and socialist society. The critical theorists developed an integrated theory of the economic, political, cultural, and psychological domination structures of advanced industrial civilization, and of the dialectic through which the emancipatory potential of modern society is suppressed and its rationality turns into a positivistic rationality of domination leading to barbarism.

Major theorists include: Max Horkheimer, Theodor W. Adorno, Walter Benjamin, Herbert Marcuse, Leo Lowental, Friedrich Pollock and Erich Fromm.

The Institute made major contributions in two areas relating to the possibility of rational human subjects, i.e. individuals who could act rationally to take charge of their own society and their own history. The first consisted of social phenomena previously considered in Marxism as part of the "superstructure" or as ideology: personality, family and authority structures (its first book publication bore the title *Studies of Authority and the Family*), and the realm of aesthetics and mass culture. Studies saw a common concern here in the ability of capitalism to destroy the preconditions of critical, revolutionary political consciousness. This meant arriving at a sophisticated awareness of the depth dimension in which social oppression sustains itself. It also meant the beginning of critical theory's recognition of ideology as part of the foundations of social structure. The Institute and various collaborators had a gigantic effect on (especially American) social science through their work *The Authoritarian Personality*, which conducted extensive empirical research, using sociological and psychoanalytic categories, in order to characterize the forces that led individuals to affiliate with or support fascist movements or parties. The study found the assertion of universals, or even truth, to be a hallmark of fascism. *The Authoritarian Personality* hypothesis which proceeded from this contributed greatly to the emergence of the counterculture. Erich Fromm, who in its initial period worked with the school, is credited with bringing it a psychoanalytic focus. However, Adorno and Horkheimer belittled Fromm's contributions, even though a central theme, "The Authoritarian Character," developed directly from Fromm's research on the subject.

The nature of Marxism itself formed the second focus of the Institute, and in this context the concept of *critical theory* originated. The term served several purposes - first, it contrasted from traditional notions of theory, which were largely either positivist or scientific. Second, the term allowed them to escape the politically charged label of "Marxism." Third, it explicitly linked them with the "critical philosophy" of Immanuel Kant, where the term "critique" meant philosophical reflection on the limits of claims made for certain kinds of knowledge and a direct connection between such critique and the emphasis on moral autonomy. In an intellectual context defined by dogmatic positivism and scientism on the one hand and dogmatic "scientific socialism" on the other, critical theory meant to rehabilitate through such a philosophically critical approach an orientation toward revolutionary agency, or at least its possibility, at a time when it seemed in decline.

Finally, in the context of both Marxist-Leninist and Social-Democratic orthodoxy, which emphasized Marxism as a new kind of positive science, they were linking up with the implicit epistemology of Karl Marx's work, which presented itself as critique, as in Marx's "Capital: a critique of political economy," wanting to emphasize that Marx was attempting to create a new kind of critical analysis oriented toward the unity of theory and revolutionary practice rather than a new kind of positive science. In the 1960s, Jürgen Habermas raised the epistemological discussion to a new level in his "Knowledge and Human Interests" (1968), by identifying critical knowledge as based on principles that differentiated it either from the natural sciences or the humanities, through its orientation to self-reflection and emancipation.

Although Horkheimer's distinction between traditional and critical theory in one sense merely repeated Marx's dictum that philosophers have always interpreted the world and the point is to change it, the Institute, in its critique of ideology, took on such philosophical currents as positivism, phenomenology, existentialism, and pragmatism, with an implied critique of contemporary Marxism, which had turned dialectics into an alternate science or metaphysics. The Institute attempted to reformulate dialectics as a concrete method, continually aware of the specific social roots of thought and of the specific constellation of forces that affected the possibility of liberation. Accordingly, critical theory rejected the materialist metaphysics of orthodox Marxism. For Horkheimer and his associates, materialism meant the orientation of theory towards practice and towards the fulfillment of human needs, not a metaphysical statement about the nature of reality.

The Second Phase

The second phase of Frankfurt School critical theory centers principally on two works that rank as classics of twentieth-century thought: Horkheimer's and Adorno's *Dialectic of Enlightenment* (1944) and Adorno's *Minima Moralia* (1951). The authors wrote both works during the Institute's American exile in the Nazi period. While retaining much of the Marxian analysis, in these works critical theory has shifted its emphasis. The critique of capitalism has turned into a critique of Western civilization as a whole. Indeed, the *Dialectic of Enlightenment* uses the *Odyssey* as a paradigm for the analysis of bourgeois consciousness. Horkheimer and Adorno already present in these works many themes that have come to dominate the social thought of recent years: the domination of nature appears as central to Western civilization long before ecology had become a catchphrase of the day.

The analysis of reason now goes one stage further. The rationality of Western civilization appears as a fusion of domination and of technological rationality, bringing all of external and internal nature under the power of the human subject.

In the process, however, the subject itself gets swallowed up, and no social force analogous to the proletariat can be identified that will enable the subject to emancipate itself. Hence the subtitle of *Minima Moralia*: "Reflections from Damaged Life." In Adorno's words,

"For since the overwhelming objectivity of historical movement in its present phase consists so far only in the dissolution of the subject, without yet giving rise to a new one, individual experience necessarily bases itself on the old subject, now historically condemned, which is still for-itself, but no longer in-itself. The subject still feels sure of its autonomy, but the nullity demonstrated to subjects by the concentration camp is already overtaking the form of subjectivity itself."

Consequently, at a time when it appears that reality itself has become ideology, the greatest contribution that critical theory can make is to explore the dialectical contradictions of individual subjective experience on the one hand, and to preserve the truth of theory on the other. Even the dialectic can become a means to domination: "Its truth or untruth, therefore, is not inherent in the method itself, but in its intention in the historical process." And this intention must be toward integral freedom and happiness: "the only philosophy which can be responsibly practiced in face of despair is the attempt to contemplate all things as they would present themselves from the standpoint of redemption." How far from orthodox Marxism is Adorno's conclusion: "But beside the demand thus placed on thought, the question of the reality or unreality of redemption itself hardly matters."

Adorno, a trained musician, wrote *The Philosophy of Modern Music*, in which he, in essence, polemicizes against beauty itself --

because it has become part of the ideology of advanced capitalist society and the false consciousness that contributes to domination by prettifying it. Avant-garde art and music preserve the truth by capturing the reality of human suffering. Hence:

"What radical music perceives is the un-transfigured suffering of man... The seismographic registration of traumatic shock becomes, at the same time, the technical structural law of music. It forbids continuity and development. Musical language is polarized according to its extreme; towards gestures of shock resembling bodily convulsions on the one hand, and on the other towards a crystalline standstill of a human being whom anxiety causes to freeze in her tracks... Modern music sees absolute oblivion as its goal. It is the surviving message of despair from the shipwrecked."

This view of modern art as producing truth only through the negation of traditional aesthetic form and traditional norms of beauty because they have become ideological is characteristic of Adorno and of the Frankfurt School generally. It has been criticized by those who do not share its conception of modern society as a false totality that renders obsolete traditional conceptions and images of beauty and harmony.

The Third Phase

From these thoughts only a short step remained to the third phase of the Frankfurt School, which coincided with the post-war period, particularly from the early 1950s to the middle 1960s. With the growth of advanced industrial society under Cold War conditions, the critical theorists recognized that the structure of capitalism and history had changed decisively, that the modes of oppression operated differently, and that the industrial working class no longer remained the determinate negation of capitalism. This led to the attempt to root the dialectic in an absolute method of negativity, as in Marcuse's *One-Dimensional Man* and Adorno's *Negative Dialectics*. During this period the Institute of Social Research re-settled in Frankfurt (although many of its associates remained in the United States), with the task not merely of continuing its research but of becoming a leading force in the sociological education and democratization of West Germany. This led to a certain systematization of the Institute's entire accumulation of empirical research and theoretical analysis.

More importantly, however, the Frankfurt School attempted to define the fate of reason in the new historical period. While Marcuse did so through analysis of structural changes in the labour process under capitalism and inherent features of the methodology of science, Horkheimer and Adorno concentrated on a re-examination of the foundation of critical theory. This effort appears in systematized form in Adorno's *Negative Dialectics*, which tries to redefine dialectics for an era in which "philosophy, which once seemed obsolete, lives on because the moment to realize it was missed." Negative dialectics expresses the idea of critical thought so conceived that the apparatus of domination cannot co-opt it. Its central notion, long a focal one for Horkheimer and Adorno, suggests that the original sin of thought lies in its attempt to eliminate all that is other than thought, the attempt by the subject to devour the object, the striving for identity. This reduction makes thought the accomplice of domination. *Negative Dialectics* rescues the "preponderance of the object," not through a naive epistemological or metaphysical realism but through a thought based on differentiation, paradox, and ruse:"a logic of disintegration." Adorno thoroughly criticizes Heidegger's fundamental ontology, which reintroduces idealistic and identity-based concepts under the guise of having overcome the philosophical tradition.

Negative Dialectics comprises a monument to the end of the tradition of the individual subject as the locus of criticism. Without a revolutionary working class, the Frankfurt School had no one to rely on but the individual subject. But, as the liberal capitalist social basis of the autonomous individual receded into the past, the dialectic based on it became more and more abstract. This stance helped prepare the way for the fourth, current phase of the Frankfurt School, shaped by the communication theory of Habermas.

Habermas's work takes the Frankfurt School's abiding interests in rationality, the human subject, democratic socialism, and the dialectical method and overcomes a set of contradictions that always weakened critical theory: the contradictions between the materialist and transcendental methods, between Marxian social theory and the individualist assumptions of critical rationalism between technical and social rationalization, and between cultural and psychological phenomena on the one hand and the economic structure of society on the other. The Frankfurt School avoided taking a stand on the precise relationship between the materialist and transcendental methods, which led to ambiguity in their writings and confusion among their readers. Habermas' epistemology synthesizes these two traditions by showing that phenomenological and transcendental analysis can be subsumed under a materialist theory of social evolution, while the materialist theory makes sense only as part of a quasi-transcendental theory of emancipatory knowledge that is the self-reflection of cultural evolution. The simultaneously empirical and transcendental nature of emancipatory knowledge becomes the foundation stone of critical theory.

By locating the conditions of rationality in the social structure of language use, Habermas moves the locus of rationality from the autonomous subject to subjects in interaction. Rationality is a property not of individuals per se, but rather of structures of undistorted communication. In this notion Habermas has overcome the ambiguous plight of the subject in critical theory. If capitalistic technological society weakens the autonomy and rationality of the subject, it is not through the domination of the individual by the apparatus but through technological rationality supplanting a describable rationality of communication. And, in his sketch of communicative ethics as the highest stage in the internal logic of the evolution of ethical systems, Habermas hints at the source of a new political practice that incorporates the imperatives of evolutionary rationality.

Frankfurt School critical theory has influenced some segments of the Left wing and leftist thought (particularly the New Left). Herbert Marcuse has occasionally been described as the theorist or intellectual progenitor of the New Left. Their critique of technology, totality, teleology and (occasionally) civilization is an influence on anarcho-primitivism. Their work also heavily influenced intellectual discourse on popular culture and scholarly popular culture studies.

Cultural Marxism

Cultural Marxism is a form of Marxism that adds an analysis of the role of the media, art, theatre, film and other cultural institutions in a society. As a form of political analysis, cultural Marxism gained strength in the 1920s, and was the model used by a group of intellectuals in Germany known as the Frankfurt School; and later by another group of intellectuals at the Centre for Contemporary

Cultural Studies in Birmingham, UK. The fields of Cultural Studies and Critical theory are rooted in (and remain influenced by) Cultural Marxism.

Background

The Frankfurt School is shorthand for the members and allies of the Institute for Social Research of the University of Frankfurt. In the 1930s the Frankfurt MSchool was forced out of Germany by the rise of the Nazi Party and moved to New York. After 1945 a number of these surviving Marxists returned to both West and East Germany. Theodor W. Adorno and Max Horkheimer were thus responsible of allowing for hibernation of cultural Marxism throughout the early years of the Cold War. In West Germany, in the late 1950s and early 1960s a revived interest in Marxism produced a new generation of Marxists engaging with the cultural transformations taking place in Fordist capitalism. One of the most prominent of these Western Marxists has been the German philosopher Wolfgang Fritz Haug.

According to UCLA professor and critical theorist Douglas Kellner, "Many 20th century Marxian theorists ranging from Georg Lukacs, Antonio Gramsci, Ernst Bloch, Walter Benjamin, and T.W. Adorno to Fredric Jameson and Terry Eagleton employed the Marxian theory to analyze cultural forms in relation to their production, their imbrications with society and history, and their impact and influences on audiences and social life." The Frankfurt School also influenced scholars such as Max Horkheimer, Wilhelm Reich, Erich Fromm and Herbert Marcuse.

Kellner explains: Cultural arxism was highly influential throughout Europe and the Western world, especially in the 1960s when Marxian thought was at its most prestigious and procreative.

Theorists like Roland Barthes and the Tel Quel group in France, Galvano Della Volpe, Lucio Colletti, and others in Italy, Fredric Jameson, Terry Eagleton, and cohort of 1960s cultural radicals in the English-speaking world, and a large number of theorists throughout the globe used cultural Marxism to develop modes of cultural studies that analyzed the production, interpretation, and reception of cultural artefacts within concrete socio-historical conditions that had contested political and ideological effects and uses. One of the most famous and influential forms of cultural studies, initially under the influence of cultural Marxism, emerged within the Centre for Contemporary Cultural Studies in Birmingham, England within a group often referred to as the Birmingham School.

Critique of Cultural Marxism

Criticism of Marcuse

Marcuse, in his 1954 book *Eros and Civilization*, argued for a politics based on the striving towards pleasure. This striving for pleasure would unite individualism, hedonism and absolute egalitarianism, because each individual would equally be able to determine their own needs and desires; thus everyone would be able to satisfy their true desires. Marcuse argues that the moral and cultural relativism of contemporary Western society impedes this egalitarian politics, because it provides no way of distinguishing between an individual's true needs, and false needs manufactured by capitalism. Paul Eidelberg, however, argues that Marcuse himself is a relativist or "nihilist," because Marcuse rejects any transcendent law or morality, and believes that all desires are morally equal. Eidelberg goes on to argue that Marcuse's nihilism leads him to call for a politicized, explicitly left-wing, academy.

Recent Criticism from the political right

Post-World War II, conservatives remained suspicious of socialism and what was called "social engineering," and some argued that Cultural Marxists and the Frankfurt School helped spark the counterculture social movements of the 1960s as part of a continuing plan of transferring Marxist subversion into cultural terms in the form of Freudo-Marxism.

Paul Gottfried in his book, *The Strange Death of Marxism*, states Marxism survived and evolved since the fall of the Soviet Union in the form of Cultural Marxism:

Neo-marxists called themselves Marxists without accepting all of Marx's historical and economic theories but while upholding socialism against capitalism, as a moral position .... Thereafter socialists would build their conceptual fabrics on Marx's notion of "alienation," extracted from his writings of the 1840s .... [They] could therefore dispense with a strictly materialist analysis and shift ... focus toward religion, morality, and aesthetics.

Is the critical observation about the Frankfurt School therefore correct, that it exemplifies 'cultural Bolshevism,' which pushes Marxist-Leninist revolution under a sociological-Freudian label? To the extent its practitioners and despisers would both answer to this characterization, it may in fact be valid ... but if Marxism under the Frankfurt School has undergone [these] alterations, then there may be little Marxism left in it. The appeal of the Critical Theorists to Marx has become increasingly ritualistic and what there is in the theory of Marxist sources is now intermingled with identifiably non-Marxist ones .... In a nutshell, they had moved beyond Marxism ... into a militantly antibourgeois stance that operates independently of Marxist economic assumptions.

Response to criticisms of Cultural Marxism

Since the early 1990s, Paleoconservatives such as Patrick Buchanan and William S. Lind have argued that "cultural Marxism" is a dominant strain in the American left, and associate with it a philosophy to 'destroy Western civilization.' Much of the critique is based on Buchanan's assertion that the Frankfurt School commandeered the American mass media, and used this cartel to infect the minds of Americans.

According to Bill Berkowitz, "It's not clear whether this diffusion of the cultural Marxism conspiracy theory into the mainstream will continue. Certainly, the anti-Semitism that underlies much of the scenario suggests that it may be repudiated in the coming years. But for now, the spread of this particular theory is a classic case of concepts that originated on the radical right slowly but surely making their way into the American mind."

The Southern Poverty Law Centre, states that "Lind's theory was one that has been pushed since the mid-1990s by the Free Congress Foundation - the idea that a small group of German philosophers, known as the Frankfurt School, had devised a cultural form of Marxism that was aimed at subverting Western civilization."

At a major Holocaust denial conference put on by veteran anti-Semite Willis Carto in Washington, D.C., Lind gave a well-received speech before some 120 "historical revisionists," conspiracy theorists, neo-Nazis and other anti-Semites, in which he identified a small group of people who he said had poisoned American culture. On this point, Lind made a powerful connection with his listeners. 'These guys,' he explained, 'were all Jewish.'

According to Richard Lichtman, a social psychology professor at the Wright Institute, the Frankfurt School is "a convenient target that very few people really know anything about...."By grounding their critique in Marxism and using the Frankfurt School, [cultural conservatives] make it seem like it's quite foreign to anything American. It takes on a mysterious cast and translates as an incomprehensible, anti-American, foreign movement that is only interested in undermining the U.S." Lichtman says that the "idea being transmitted is that we are being infected from the outside."

9

Autonomist Marxism

Autonomism refers to a set of left-wing political and social movements and theories close to the socialist movement. Autonomism (*autonomia*), as an identifiable theoretical system, first emerged in Italy in the 1960s from workerist (*operaismo*) communism. Later, post-Marxist and anarchist tendencies became significant after influence from the Situationists, the failure of the Italian far-left movements in the 1970s and the emergence of a number of important theorists including Antonio Negri, who had contributed to the 1969 founding of *Potere Operaio* Marxist group, Mario Tronti, Paolo Virno, etc. It influenced the German and Dutch Autonomen, the worldwide Social Centre movement, and today is influential in Italy, France, and to a significantly lesser extent the English-speaking countries. Those who describe themselves as autonomists now vary from Marxists to post-structuralists and (some) anarchists.

Etymology

The term *autonomia/Autonome* is derived from the Greek word referring to someone or something which lives by his/her own rule.

Autonomy, in this sense, is not independence. While independence refers to an autarkic kind of life, separated from the community, autonomy refers to life in society but by one's own rule. Aristotle thus considered that only beasts or gods could be independent and live apart from the *polis* ("community"), while Kant defined the Enlightenment by autonomy of thought and the famous *"Sapere aude"* ("dare to know.)"

The Marxist Autonomist theory

Unlike other forms of Marxism, autonomist Marxism emphasises the ability of the working class to force changes to the organisation of the capitalist system independent of the state, trade unions or political parties. Autonomists are less concerned with party political organisation than other Marxists, focusing instead on self-organised action outside of traditional organisational structures. Autonomist Marxism is thus a "bottom up" theory: it draws attention to activities that autonomists see as everyday working class resistance to capitalism, for example absenteeism, slow working, and socialisation in the workplace.

Like other Marxists, autonomists see class struggle as being of central importance. However, autonomists have a broader definition of the working class than other Marxists: as well as wage-earning workers (both white collar and blue collar), autonomists also include the unwaged (students, the unemployed, homemakers etc), who are traditionally deprived of any form of union representation.

Early theorists (such as Mario Tronti, Antonio Negri, Sergio Bologna and Paolo Virno) developed notions of "immaterial" and "social labour" that extended the Marxist concept of labour to all society. They suggested that modern society's wealth was produced by unaccountable collective work, and that only a little of this was redistributed to the workers in the form of wages. They emphasised the importance of feminism and the value of unpaid female labour to capitalist society.

Italian Autonomism

Autonomist Marxism - referred to in Italy as *operaismo*, which translates literally as "workerism" - first appeared in Italy in the early 1960s. Arguably, the emergence of early autonomism can be traced to the dissatisfaction of automotive workers in Turin with their union, which reached an agreement with FIAT. The disillusionment of these workers with their organised representation, along with the resultant riots (in particular the 1962 riots by FIAT workers in Turin - "fatti di Piazza Statuto") were critical factors in the development of a theory of self-organised labour representation outside the scope of traditional representatives such as trade unions.

In 1969, the *operaismo* approach was active mainly in two different groups: *Lotta Continua*, led by Adriano Sofri (which had a very significant Roman Catholic cultural matrix) and *Potere Operaio*, led by Antonio Negri, Franco Piperno, Oreste Scalzone, and Valerio Morucci. Mario Capanna was the charismatic leader of the Milan student movement, which had a more classical Marxist-Leninist approach.

Influences

Through translations made available by Danilo Montaldi and others, the Italian autonomists drew upon previous activist research in the United States by the Johnson-Forest Tendency and in France by the group Socialisme ou Barbarie (see below). The Johnson-Forest Tendency had studied working class life and struggles within the US auto industry, publishing pamphlets such as "The American Worker" (1947), "Punching Out" (1952) and "Union Committeemen and Wildcat Strikes" (1955). That work was translated into French by Socialisme ou Barbarie and published, serially, in their journal. They too began investigating and writing about what was going on inside workplaces, in their case inside both auto factories and insurance offices.

The journal *Quaderni Rossi* ("Red Notebooks"), along with its successor *Classe Operaia* ("Working Class"), were also influential in the development of early autonomism. Both of these were founded by Antonio Negri and Mario Tronti - Quaderni Rossi was produced between 1961 and 1965, and Classe Operaia between 1963 and 1966.

Pirate radio stations also were a factor in spreading autonomist ideas and theory. Bologna's Radio Alice was an example of such a station.

Direct action

The Italian student movement, starting from 1966 (murder by neo-fascists of student Paolo Rossi in Rome University) engaged in various direct action operations, including riots and University occupations, along with more peaceful activities such as self reduction, in which individuals refused to pay for such services and goods as public transport, electricity, gas, rent, and food. Several clashes occurred between the students ("Movimento studentesco") and the police, during the occupations of Universities in the winter 1967-1968, during the Fiat occupations, in March 1968 in Rome during the "Battle of Valle Giulia".

The Piazza Fontana bombing and its legacy

In December 1969, four bombings struck in Rome the Monument of Vittorio Emanuele II (*Altare della Patria*), the *Banca Nazionale del Lavoro*, and in Milan the *Banca Commerciale* and the *Banca Nazionale dell'Agricoltura*. The latter bombing, known as the Piazza Fontana bombing of 12 December 1969, killed 16 and injured 90, conventionally marking the beginning of the "strategia della tensione" (strategy of tension) in Italy. After the bombing, numerous members of left-wing groups - including anarchists - were detained by the police. Giuseppe Pinelli, an anarchist, was accused at the time of having carried out the bombing.

Giuseppe Pinelli was held and interrogated for three days, longer than Italian law specified that people could be held without seeing a judge. On December 15, he died after falling out of a window. Luigi Calabresi, the police officer who had directed his interrogation, as well as other officers were accused of pushing him out of the window, and put under investigation in 1971 for murder, but charges were dropped because of lack of evidence. The next year, Calabresi was murdered by two shots from a revolver outside his home.

Another anarchist, Pietro Valpreda, was arrested, sentenced for the crime, before being released and eventually cleared sixteen years later. In the 1980s, the neo-fascist terrorist Vincenzo Vinciguerra confessed to magistrate Felice Casson that the bombing had in fact been carried out by the far-right organisation *Ordine Nuovo*, supported by Gladio, NATO's stay-behind anti-Communist network, in an attempt to push the state into declaring a state of emergency. All defendants were acquitted by the Court of Cassation on May 3, 2005, during the seventh trial for the Piazza Fontana bombing.

This attack has been widely considered part of the strategy of tension (*strategia della tensione*), which allegedly aimed at destabilizing the country through a campaign of "false flags" terrorist attacks - attacks blamed on left-wing groups. The strategy aimed to promote an authoritarian government and (in later years) to sabotage the possibilities for a historic compromise (*compromesso storico*) between the Christian Democracy (DC) and the Communist Party (PCI).

In 1988, former *Lotta continua* member Adriano Sofri was arrested, along with Ovidio Bompressi and Giorgio Pietrostefani, for the murder of Luigi Calabresi, the police officer who was suspected of having killed Giuseppe Pinelli. The charges against them were based on the violent press campaign conducted by Lotta Continua against Calabresi, on testimony provided, sixteen years after the facts, by a "collabouratore di giustizia"- an ex-militant who contacted police authorities and accused himself of having carried out the murder of Calabresi (under order from Sofri) and collabourated with the magistrates. Sofri claimed his innocence, but was sentenced after a long series of trials, in 2000. Historian Carlo Ginzburg wrote, on this case, a book in support of Sofri's innocence, entitled *The Judge and the Historian: Marginal Notes on a Late Twentieth-Century Miscarriage of Justice.*

The killing of Aldo Moro and the prosecution of the autonomists
On March 11, 1977, riots took place in Bologna following the killing of a young man by the police.

Starting from 1979, the state effectively prosecuted the autonomist movement, claiming it protected the Red Brigades, which had kidnapped and assassinated Aldo Moro. 12, 000 far-left activists were detained; 600 fled the country, including 300 to France and 200 others to South America..

The French Autonome movement

In France, the Marxist group *Socialisme ou Barbarie*, led by philosopher Cornelius Castoriadis, could be said to be one of the first autonomist groups, as well as having importance in the council communist tradition. As mentioned above, *Socialisme ou Barbarie* drew upon the American Johnson-Forest Tendency's activist research inside US auto plants and carried out their own investigations into rank and file workers struggles - struggles autonomous of union or party leadership.

Also parallel to the work of the Johnson-Forest Tendency, *Socialisme ou Barbarie* harshly criticised the Stalinist regime in the USSR, which it considered a form of 'bureaucratic capitalism' and not at all the state socialism it pretended to be. Philosopher Jean-François Lyotard, famous for his work on post-modernism, was also part of this movement.

However, the Italian influence of the *operaismo* movement was more directly felt in the creation of the review *Matériaux pour l'intervention* (1972-1973) by Yann Moulier-Boutang, a French economist close to Toni Negri. This led in turn to the creation of the *Camarades* group (1974-78) by Moulier-Boutang. Along with others, Moulier-Boutang joined the *Centre International pour des Nouveaux Espaces de Liberté* (CINEL), founded three years before by Félix Guattari, and assisted Italian activists accused of terrorism, of whom at least 300 fled to France.

The French autonome mouvement organised itself in the AGPA (*Assemblée Parisienne des Groupes Autonomes*, "Parisian Assembly of Autonome Groups;" 1977-78). Many tendencies were present in it, including the *Camarades* group led by Moulier-Boutang, members of the *Organisation communiste libertaire* (OCL

- an autonomist group), some people referring themselves to the "Desiring Autonomy" of Bob Nadoulek, but also squatters and street-wise people (including the *groupe Marge*). French autonomes supported captured Rote Armee Fraktion ("Red Army Faction" — RAF) terrorists. Jean-Paul Sartre also intervened on the conditions for the detention of RAF detainees.

The militant group *Action Directe* appeared in 1979 and carried out several violent direct actions. Action Directe claimed responsibility for the murders of Renault's CEO Georges Besse and General Audran. George Besse had been CEO of nuclear company Eurodif. *Action Directe* was dissolved in 1987.

In the 1980s, the autonomist movement underwent a deep crisis in Italy because of effective prosecution by the State, and was stronger in Germany than in France. It remained present in Parisian squats and in some riots (for example in 1980 near the Jussieu campus in Paris, or in 1982 in the Ardennes department during anti-nuclear demonstrations). In the 1980s, the French autonomists published the periodicals *CAT Pages* (1981-1982), *Rebelles* (1981-1993), *Tout!* (1982-1985), *Molotov et Confetti* (1984), *Les Fossoyeurs du Vieux Monde, La Chôme* (1984-1985) and *Contre* (1987-1989).

In the 1990s, the French autonomist movement was present in struggles led by unemployed people, with *Travailleurs, Chômeurs, et Précaires en colère* (TCP, "Angry Workers, Unemployed, and Precarious people") and *l'Assemblée générale des chômeurs de Jussieu* ("General Assembly of Jussieu's unemployed people.)" It was also involved in the alter-globalisation movement and above all in the solidarity with illegal foreigners (Collective Des Papiers pour tous ("Permits for all," 1996) and *Collectif Anti-Expulsion* (1998-

2005)). Several autonomist journals date from this time: *Quilombo* (1988-1993), *Apache* (1990-1998), *Tic-Tac* (1995-1997), *Karoshi* (1998-1999), and *Tiqqun* (1999-2001).

From July 19 to July 28, 2002, a No Borders camp was made in Strasbourg to protest against anti-immigration policies, in particular inside the Schengen European space.

In 2003, autonomists came into conflict with the French Socialist Party (PS) during a demonstration that took place in the frame of the European Social Forum in Saint-Denis (Paris). At the end of December, hundreds of unemployed people helped themselves in the *Bon Marché* supermarket to be able to celebrate Christmas (an action called *"autoréduction"* (of prices) in French). French riot police (CRS) physically opposed the unemployed people inside the shop. Autonomes rioted during the spring 2006 protests against the CPE, and again after the 2007 presidential election when Nicolas Sarkozy was elected.

The German Autonome movement in the 1970-80s

In Germany, Autonome was used during the late 1970s to depict the most radical part of the political left. These individuals participated in practically all actions of the social movements at the time, especially in demonstrations against nuclear energy plants (Brokdorf 1981, Wackersdorf 1986) and in actions against the construction of airport runways (Frankfurt 1976-1986). The defence of squats against the police such as in Hamburg's *Hafenstraße* was also a major "task" for the "autonome" movement. The Dutch anarchist *Autonomen* movement from the 1960s also concentrated on squatting.

Tactics of the "Autonome" were usually militant, including the construction of barricades or throwing stones or molotov cocktails at the police. During their most powerful times in the early 1980s, on at least one occasion the police had to take flight.

Because of their outfit (heavy black clothing, ski masks, helmets), the "Autonome" were dubbed *der schwarze Block* by the German media, and in these tactics were similar to modern black blocs. In 1989, laws regarding demonstrations in Germany were changed, prohibiting the use of so-called "passive weaponry" such as helmets or padding and covering your face.

Today, the "autonome" scene in Germany is greatly reduced and concentrates mainly on anti-fascist actions, ecology, solidarity with refugees, and feminism. There are larger and more militant groups still in operation, such as in Switzerland or Italy.

The Greek Anarcho-autonomoi

In Greece, the "anarcho-autonomoi" ("anarchists-autonomists") emerged as an important trend in the youth and student's movement, first during the 1973 Athens Polytechnic uprising against the military dictatorship which at that time ruled the country. After the collapse of the dictatorship in 1974, the "anarcho-autonomoi" became considerably influential, firstly as a social trend within the youth and then as a (very loose and diverse) political trend. The definition "anarcho-autonomoi," itself, is much debated. One reason for this is that it was originally coined by opponents. However, it was also quite quickly adopted by many adherents, used as a generic term. - Before 1973, in Greece, there was very little tradition in Anarchism or Libertarian Socialism in general. An exception to this was Agis Stinas, an early comrade of Cornelius Castoriadis. Castoriadis belonged to Stinas's small Council Communist group (before he immigrated to France) and was influenced by it (later these roles were turned around). Such small groups which existed, were almost (physically) eliminated by the Nazis, the local establishment and the Stalinist communist party during the Nazi occupation and the Greek Civil War that followed, with Castoriadis and Stinas, themselves, being two of the few survivors. Thus, the radical Greek youth in the 70s, having very little relative background to refer to, resided to an extensive "syncretism" of multiple trends originating in the respective movements in other European countries. Anarchist and anarcho-syndicalist trends did converge with situationist, workerist or other autonomist trends and even with radical (non-autonomist) Marxist trends. The "anarcho-autonomoi" made a very strong stand during the 1978-80 student movement, coming also into violent confrontation with the police and the (also, of considerable influence) Stalinist communist youth (K.N.E). Such stands were repeated again and again whenever the student's, the worker's and the youth movement were at a rise (in 1987, in 1990-91, in 1998-99, in 2006-07). However, their intensity has been falling since after 1990-91. - Parallel to such participation in social movements a large number of social-centres (many of them squatted) exist, to the day, around Greece and many of them participate in social struggles on a more local level. These social centers, whether they identify, now, as "Autonomist" or not (most use more generic terms as "anti-authoritarian," some identify as "anarchist"), function in the ways that historically emerged through "Autonomia". - There is also a multitude of small political groups which identify as "Autonomist" (ranging from workerist to post-modernist). Most of them are still connected to the respective groups that identify as "Anarchist."

Influence

The Autonomist Marxist and *Autonomen* movements provided inspiration to some on the revolutionary left in English speaking countries, particularly among anarchists, many of whom have adopted autonomist tactics. Some English-speaking anarchists even describe themselves as *Autonomists*. The Italian *operaismo* movement also influenced Marxist academics such as Harry Cleaver, John Holloway, Steve Wright, and Nick Dyer-Witheford. In Denmark, the word is used as a catch-all phrase for anarchists and the extra parliamentary extreme left in general, as was seen in the media coverage of the eviction of the Ungdomshuset squat in Copenhagen in March 2007.

10

Analytical Marxism

Analytical Marxism refers to a style of thinking about Marxism that was prominent amongst English-speaking philosophers and social scientists during the 1980s. It was mainly associated with the September Group of academics, so called because of their biennial September meetings to discuss common interests. The group also dubbed itself "Non-Bullshit Marxism," and was characterized, in the words of David Miller, by "clear and rigorous thinking about questions that are usually blanketed by ideological fog." The most prominent members of the group were G. A. Cohen, John Roemer, Jon Elster, Adam Przeworski, Erik Olin Wright, Philippe van Parijs, and Robert-Jan van der Veen.

Origin

Analytical Marxism is usually understood to have taken off with the publication of G. A. Cohen's *Karl Marx's Theory of History: A Defence* (1978). More broadly conceived, it might be seen as having originated in the post-war period in the work of political philosophers such as Karl Popper, H. B. Acton, and John Plamenatz, who employed the techniques of analytical philosophy in order to test the coherence and scientific validity of Marxism as a theory of history and society.

Those thinkers were critical of Marxism. Cohen's book was, from the outset, intended as a defence of historical materialism. Cohen painstakingly reconstructed historical materialism through a close reading of Marx's texts, with the aim of providing the most logically coherent and parsimonious account. For Cohen, Marx's historical materialism is a technologically deterministic theory, in which the economic relations of production are functionally explained by the material forces of production, and in which the political and legal institutions (the "superstructure") are functionally explained by the relations of production (the "base)". The transition from one mode of production to another is driven by the tendency of the productive forces to develop. Cohen accounts for this tendency by reference to the rational character of the human species: where there is the opportunity to adopt a more productive technology and thus reduce the burden of labour, human beings will tend to take it. Thus, human history can be understood as the gradual development of human productive power.

September Group

The *September Group* (also known as the *No-Bullshit Marxism Group*) is a small circle of scholars interested in Analytical Marxism. Its original members included G.A. Cohen, Jon Elster, Adam Przeworski, Erik Olin Wright, Robert Brenner, Hillel Steiner, Philippe Van Parijs, Robert Van Der Veen, Samuel Bowles and John Roemer. The group, so-called because it traditionally meets in September, reconvenes every other year in varying locations. Meetings are usually also attended by a guest scholar who is not a permanent member of the group.

Although all the members of the September Group share an interest in Marxism, some of them, like Van Parijs and Steiner, have never described themselves as Marxists. Elster and Przeworski were notable departures from the group in the early 1990s. Latecomers include Thomas Piketty and, more recently, Joshua Cohen.

Theory

Exploitation

At the same time as Cohen was working on *Karl Marx's Theory of History*, American economist John Roemer was employing neoclassical economics in order to try to defend the Marxist concepts of exploitation and class. In his *General Theory of Exploitation and Class* (1982), Roemer employed rational choice and game theory in order to demonstrate how exploitation and class relations may arise in the development of a market for labour. Roemer would go on to reject the idea that the labour theory of value was necessary for explaining exploitation and class. Value was in principle capable of being explained in terms of any class of commodity inputs, such as oil, wheat, etc., rather than being exclusively explained by embodied labour power. Roemer was led to the conclusion that exploitation and class were thus generated not in the sphere of production but of market exchange. Significantly, as a purely technical category, exploitation did not always imply a moral wrong (see section Justice below).

Rational Choice Marxism

By the mid-1980s, "analytical Marxism" was being recognised as a "paradigm." The September group had been meeting for several years, and a succession of texts by its members were published. Several of these appeared under the imprint of Cambridge University Press's series "Studies in Marxism and Social Theory," including Jon Elster's *Making Sense of Marx* (1985) and Adam Przeworski's *Capitalism and Social Democracy* (1986). Elster's account was an exhaustive trawl through Marx's texts in order to ascertain what could be salvaged out of Marxism employing the tools of rational choice theory and methodological individualism (which Elster defended as the only form of explanation appropriate to the social sciences). His conclusion was that - contra Cohen - no general theory of history as the development of the productive forces could be saved. Like Roemer, he also rejected the labour theory of value and, going further, virtually all of Marx's economics. The "dialectical" method is savaged as a form of Hegelian obscurantism. The theory of ideology and revolution continued to be useful to a certain degree, but only once they had been purged of their tendencies to holism and functionalism and established on the basis of an individualist methodology and a causal or intentional explanation.

Przeworski's book uses rational choice and game theory in order to demonstrate that the revolutionary strategies adopted by socialists in the twentieth century were likely to fail, since it was in the rational interests of workers to strive for the reform of capitalism through the achievement of union recognition, improved wages and living conditions, rather than adopting the risky strategy of revolution. Przeworski's book is clearly influenced by economic explanations of political behaviour advanced by thinkers such as Anthony Downs (*An Economic Theory of Democracy*, 1957) and Mancur Olson (*The Logic of Collective Action*, 1971).

Justice

The analytical (and rational choice) Marxists held a variety of leftist political sympathies, ranging from communism to reformist social democracy. Through the 1980s, most of them began to believe that Marxism as a theory capable of explaining revolution in terms of the economic dynamics of capitalism and the class interests of the proletariat had been seriously compromised. They were largely in agreement that the transformation of capitalism was an ethical project. During the 1980s, a debate had developed within Anglophone academia about whether Marxism could accommodate a theory of justice. This debate was clearly linked to the revival of normative political philosophy after the publication of John Rawls's *A Theory of Justice* (1971). Some commentators remained hostile to the idea of a Marxist theory of justice, arguing that Marx saw "justice" as little more than a bourgeois ideological construct designed to justify exploitation by reference to reciprocity in the wage contract. The analytical Marxists, however, largely rejected this point of view. Led by G. A. Cohen (a moral philosopher by training), they argued that a Marxist theory of justice had to focus on egalitarianism. For Cohen, this meant an engagement with moral and political philosophy in order to demonstrate the injustice of market exchange, and the construction of an appropriate egalitarian metric. This argument is pursued in Cohen's most recent books, *Self-Ownership, Freedom and Equality* (1995) and *If You're an Egalitarian How Come You're So Rich?* (2000b).

Cohen departs from some previous Marxists by arguing that capitalism is a system characterised by unjust exploitation not because the labour of workers is "stolen" by employers, but because it is a system wherein "autonomy" is infringed and which results in a distribution of benefits and burdens that is unfair. In the traditional Marxist account, exploitation and injustice occur because non-workers appropriate the value produced by the labour of workers, something that would be overcome in a socialist society wherein no class would own the means of production and be in a position to appropriate the value produced by labourers. Cohen argues that underpinning this account is the assumption that workers have "rights of self-ownership" over themselves and thus, should "own" what is produced by their labour. Because the worker is paid a wage less than the value he or she creates through work, the capitalist is said to extract a surplus-value from the worker's labour, and thus to steal part of what the worker produces, the time of the worker and the worker's powers.

Cohen argues that the concept of self-ownership is favourable to Rawls's difference principle as it ensures "each person's rights over his being and powers" - i.e. that one is treated as an end always and never as a means - but also highlights that its centrality provides for an area of common ground between the Marxist account of justice and the right-wing libertarianism of Robert Nozick. However, much as Cohen criticises Rawls for treating people's personal powers as just another external resource for which no individual can claim desert, so does he charge Nozick with moving beyond the *concept* of self-ownership to his own right-wing "thesis" of self-ownership. In Cohen's view, Nozick's mistake is to endow people's claims to legitimately acquire external resources with the same moral quality that belongs to people's ownership of themselves. In other words, libertarianism allows inequalities to arise from differences in talent and differences in external resources, but it does so because it assumes that the world is "up for grabs," i.e. can be justly appropriated as private property, with virtually no restriction(s).

Criticisms

Analytical Marxism came under fire from a number of different quarters, both Marxist and non-Marxist.

Method

A number of critics argued that analytical Marxism proceeded from the wrong methodological and epistemological premises. While the analytical Marxists dismissed dialectically oriented Marxism as "bullshit," many Marxists would maintain that the distinctive character of Marxist philosophy is lost if it is understood non-dialectically. The crucial feature of Marxist philosophy is that it is not a reflection in thought of the world, a crude materialism, but rather an intervention in the world concerned with human praxis. According to this view, analytical Marxism wrongly characterises intellectual activity as occurring in isolation from the struggles constitutive of its social and political conjuncture, and at the same time does little to intervene in that conjuncture. For dialectical Marxists, analytical Marxism eviscerated Marxism, turning it from a systematic doctrine of revolutionary transformation into a set of discrete theses that stand or fall on the basis of their logical consistency and empirical validity.

Analytical Marxism's non-Marxist critics also objected to its methodological weaknesses. Against Elster and the rational choice Marxists, it was argued that methodological individualism was not the only form of valid explanation in the social sciences, that functionalism in the absence of micro-foundations could remain a convincing and fruitful mode of inquiry, and that rational choice and game theory were far from being universally accepted as sound or useful ways of modeling social institutions and processes.

History

Cohen's defence of a technological determinist interpretation of historical materialism was, in turn, quite widely criticised, even by analytical Marxists. Together with Andrew Levine, Wright argued that in attributing primacy to the productive forces (the development thesis), Cohen overlooked the role played by class actors in the transition between modes of production. For the authors, it was forms of class relations (the relations of production) that had primacy in terms of how the productive forces were employed and the extent to which they developed. It was not evident, they claimed, that the relations of production become "fetters" once the productive forces are capable of sustaining a different set of production relations. Other non-Marxist critics argued that Cohen, in line with the Marxist tradition, underestimated the role played by the legal and political superstructure in shaping the character of the economic base. Finally, Cohen's anthropology was judged dubious: whether human beings adopt new and more productive technology is not a function of an ahistorical rationality, but depends on the extent to which these forms of technology are compatible with pre-existing beliefs and social practices. Cohen recognised and accepted some, though not all, of these criticisms in his *History, Labour, and Freedom* (1988).

Justice and Power

Many Marxists would argue that Marxism cannot be understood as a theory of justice in the sense intended by the analytical Marxists. The question of justice cannot be seen in isolation from questions of power, or from the balance of class forces in any specific conjuncture. Non-Marxists may employ a similar criticism in their critique of liberal theories of justice in the Rawlsian tradition. They argue that the theories fail to address problems about the configuration of power relations in the contemporary world, and by so doing appear as little more than exercises in logic. "Justice," on this view, is whatever is produced by the assumptions of the theory. It has little to do with the actual distribution of power and resources in the world.

Karl Marx

11

Marxist Humanism

Marxist humanism is a branch of Marxism that primarily focuses on Marx's earlier writings, especially the *Economic and Philosophical Manuscripts of 1844* in which Marx espoused his theory of alienation, as opposed to his later works, which are considered to be concerned more with his structural conception of capitalist society. The Praxis School, which called for radical social change in Josip Broz Tito's Yugoslavia in the 1960s, was one such Marxist humanist movement.

Marxist humanism was opposed by the "anti-humanism" of Marxist philosopher Louis Althusser, who qualified it as a revisionist movement.

The theory of "Marxist Humanism"

The term "Marxist humanism" has as its foundation Marx's conception of the "alienation of the labourer" as he advanced it in his *Economic and Philosophic Manuscripts of 1844* -- an alienation that is born of a capitalist system in which the worker no longer functions as (what Marx termed) a free being involved with free and associated labour. And although many scholars consider late

Marx less of a humanist than the Marx who wrote pre-*Das Kapital* (For Marx by Althusser), as his later works are rather bereft of references to this alienation, others {for example David McLellan, Robert C. Tucker, George Brenkert}argue that the notion of alienation remains a part of Marx's philosophy. Theodor Shanin) and Raya Dunayevskaya go further, not only is alienation present in the late Marx, but that there is no split between the young Marx and mature Marx, but one Marx.

As is assumed under the very notion of alienation, there is a human who, when disenfranchised by his own labour, becomes less human - in fact, Marx says he becomes objectified. According to Marx, humans naturally produce for their own benefit; and, furthermore, he freely produces in association with other free beings. However, under a capitalist society the alienation of the means of production gives rise to "fettering" productive relations; there is a single capitalist employing an army of workers at wages just sufficient to provide for their mere subsistence. The worker becomes a slave. He is no longer a free productive being, but instead he absolutely must produce to simply meet his most basic needs. Multiple alienations are evident: from themselves, from the human being, from the object they produce, and the process of work itself. The stamp of Hegel is clear and unmistakable.

However, there is more to this. In his *Economic and Philosophic Manuscripts* Marx writes: "A forcing-up of wages (disregarding all other difficulties, including the fact that it would only be by force, too, that the higher-wages, being an anomaly, could be maintained) would therefore be nothing but better payment for the slave, and would not conquer either for the worker or for labour their human status and dignity." It is here that Marx as a humanist is well evinced.

This quote is intended to convey that it is not the 12-hour work-day alone that enslaves man, forcing him to give his entire productive being -- his natural skills, or that which constitutes his essence as a man -- over to another. Rather, it is the very (philosophic) condition behind the capitalist structure that enslaves man. Basically, capitalism is not conducive to democracy on Marx's conception. On his conception, capitalism inherently gives rise to an elite bourgeoisie for whom the rest of society, the proletariat, must work. Insofar as this is the case, the proletarian himself will never be able to dictate the conditions of his work; they will always be determined by the capitalist himself. So, even if the capitalist pays the worker higher wages than he himself incurs (from his profits made off the labourer's efforts), he still controls the terms of the worker's production.

Marx held that insofar as man only has his liberty to produce, and produce according to his own conceived ideas (*e.g.*, he designs a very fancy shoe and wants to see this shoe materialize), capitalism, as a system, will be an eternal stymie to man's natural freedom.

This is Marx's humanism. Marxist Humanism is the political, or philosophic, association that assumes this as its premise.

Criticism

The most potent criticism of Marxist Humanism has come from within the Marxist movement. Louis Althusser, the French Structuralist Marxist, criticises Marxist Humanists for not recognising the dichotomy between 'Young Marx' and 'Mature Marx.' Of the Humanist's reliance on the 1844 *Economic and Philosophic Manuscripts* Althusser wrote, "We do not publish our own drafts, that is, our own mistakes, but we do sometimes publish other people's" (cited in Gregory Elliot's "introduction: In the

Mirror of Machiavelli" an introduction for Althusser's "Machiavelli and us", p. xi). The Humanists contend that 'Marxism' developed lopsidedly because Marx's early works were unknown until after the orthodox ideas were in vogue - the Manuscripts of 1844 were published only in 1932 - and to understand his latter works properly it is necessary to understand Marx's philosophical foundations. Althusser, however, did not defend orthodox Marxism's economic reductionism and determinism; instead, he developed his own theories regarding ideological hegemony and conditioning within class societies, through the concept of Ideological State Apparatuses (ISA) and interpellation which constitutes the subject.

Marxist theology

Although Marx was intensely critical of institutionalized religion including Christianity, some Christians accepted the basic premises of Marxism and re-interpreted their faith from this perspective. Some of the resulting examples are liberation theology and black liberation theology. Pope Benedict XVI strongly opposed radical liberation theology while he was still a cardinal, with the Vatican condemning acceptance of Marxism. Black liberation theologian James Cone wrote in his book *For My People* that "for analyzing the structure of capitalism. Marxism as a tool of social analysis can disclose the gap between appearance and reality, and thereby help Christians to see how things really are."

12

Key Western Marxists

Georg Lukács

Georg Lukács (April 13, 1885 - June 4, 1971) was a Hungarian
Marxist philosopher and literary critic in the tradition of Western
Marxism. His main work *History and Class Consciousness* (written
between 1919 and 1922 and first published in 1923), initiated the
current of thought that came to be known as Western Marxism.
The book is notable for contributing to debates concerning
Marxism and its relation to sociology, politics and philosophy and
for reconstructing Marx's theory of alienation before many of the
works of the Young Marx had been published. Lukács's work
elaborates and expands upon Marxist theories such as ideology,
false consciousness, reification and class consciousness.

Karl Korsch

Karl Korsch (August 15, 1886 - October 21, 1961) was born in
Tostedt, near Hamburg, to the family of a middle-ranking bank
official.

In his later work, he rejected orthodox (classical) Marxism as
historically outmoded, wanting to adapt Marxism to a new

historical situation. He wrote in his *Ten Theses* (1950) that "the first step in re-establishing a revolutionary theory and practice consists in breaking with that Marxism which claims to monopolize revolutionary initiative as well as theoretical and practical direction" and that "today, all attempts to re-establish the Marxist doctrine as a whole in its original function as a theory of the working classes social revolution are reactionary utopias."

Korsch was especially concerned that Marxist theory was losing its precision and validity - in the words of the day, becoming "vulgarized" - within the upper echelons of the various socialist organizations. His masterwork, *Marxism and Philosophy* is an attempt to re-establish the historic character of Marxism as the heir to Hegel.

Antonio Gramsci

Antonio Gramsci (January 22, 1891 - April 27, 1937) was an Italian writer, politician and political theorist. He was a founding member and onetime leader of the Communist Party of Italy. Gramsci can be seen as one of the most important Marxist thinkers of the twentieth century, and in particular a key thinker in the development of Western Marxism. He wrote more than 30 notebooks and 3000 pages of history and analysis during his imprisonment. These writings, known as the *Prison Notebooks*, contain Gramsci's tracing of Italian history and nationalism, as well as some ideas in Marxist theory, critical theory and educational theory associated with his name, such as:

- Cultural hegemony as a means of maintaining the state in a capitalist society.

- The need for popular workers' education to encourage development of intellectuals from the working class.

- The distinction between political society (the police, the army, legal system, etc.) which dominates directly and coercively, and civil society (the family, the education system, trade unions, etc.) where leadership is constituted through ideology or by means of consent.

- 'Absolute historicism.'

- The critique of economic determinism.

- The critique of philosophical materialism.

Herbert Marcuse

Herbert Marcuse (July 19, 1898 - July 29, 1979) was a prominent German-American philosopher and sociologist of Jewish descent, and a member of the Frankfurt School.

Marcuse's critiques of capitalist society (especially his 1955 synthesis of Marx and Freud, *Eros and Civilization*, and his 1964 book *One-Dimensional Man*) resonated with the concerns of the leftist student movement in the 1960s. Because of his willingness to speak at student protests, Marcuse soon became known as "the father of the New Left," a term he disliked and rejected.

Jean-Paul Sartre

Jean-Paul Sartre (June 21, 1905 - April 15, 1980) was already a key and influential philosopher and playwright for his early writings on individualistic existentialism. In his later career, he attempted to reconcile the existential philosophy of Søren Kierkegaard with Marxist philosophy and Hegelian dialectics in his work *Critique of Dialectical Reason*.

Sartre was also involved in Marxist politics and was impressed upon visiting Marxist revolutionary Che Guevara, calling him "not only an intellectual but also the most complete human being of our age."

Louis Althusser

Louis Althusser (October 16, 1918 - October 22, 1990) was a Marxist philosopher. He was a lifelong member and sometimes strong critic of the French Communist Party. His arguments and theses were set against the threats that he saw attacking the theoretical foundations of Marxism. These included both the influence of empiricism on Marxist theory, and humanist and reformist socialist orientations which manifested as divisions in the European Communist Parties, as well as the problem of the 'cult of personality' and of ideology itself. Althusser is commonly referred to as a Structural Marxist, although his relationship to other schools of French structuralism is not a simple affiliation and he is critical of many aspects of structuralism.

His essay *Marxism and Humanism* is a strong statement of anti-humanism in Marxist theory, condemning ideas like "human potential" and "species-being," which are often put forth by Marxists, as outgrowths of a bourgeois ideology of "humanity." His essay *Contradiction and Overdetermination* borrows the concept of over determination from psychoanalysis, in order to replace the idea of "contradiction" with a more complex model of multiple causality in political situations (an idea closely related to Antonio Gramsci's concept of hegemony).

Althusser is also widely known as a theorist of ideology, and his best-known essay is *Ideology and Ideological State Apparatuses: Notes Toward an Investigation*. The essay establishes the concept of ideology, also based on Gramsci's theory of hegemony. Whereas hegemony is ultimately determined entirely by political forces, ideology draws on Freud's and Lacan's concepts of the unconscious and mirror-phase respectively, and describes the structures and systems that allow us to meaningfully have a concept of the self.

Hill, Hobsbawm, and Thompson

British Marxism deviated sharply from French (especially Althusserian) Marxism and, like the Frankfurt School, developed an attention to cultural experience and an emphasis on human agency while growing increasingly distant from determinist views of materialism. A circle of historians inside the Communist Party of Great Britain (CPGB) formed the Communist Party Historians Group in 1946. They shared a common interest in 'history from below' and class structure in early capitalist society. Important members of the group included E.P. Thompson, Eric Hobsbawm, Christopher Hill and Raphael Samuel.

While some members of the group (most notably E.P. Thompson) left the CPGB after the 1956 Hungarian Revolution, the common points of British Marxist historiography continued in their works. They placed a great emphasis on the subjective determination of history. E. P. Thompson famously engaged Althusser in *The Poverty of Theory*, arguing that Althusser's theory overdetermined history, and left no space for historical revolt by the oppressed.

Post Marxism

Post-Marxism represents the theoretical work of philosophers and social theorists who have built their theories upon those of Marx and Marxists but exceeded the limits of those theories in ways that puts them outside of Marxism. It begins with the basic tenets of Marxism but moves away from the Mode of Production as the starting point for analysis and includes factors other than class, such as gender, ethnicity etc, and a reflexive relationship between the base and superstructure.

Marxism remains a powerful theory in some unexpected and relatively obscure places, and is not always properly labeled as "Marxism." For example, many Mexican and some American archaeologists still cling to a Marxist model to explain the Classic Maya Collapse (c. 900 A.D.) - without mentioning Marxism by name.

Marxist Feminism

Marxist feminism is a sub-type of feminist theory which focuses on the dismantling of capitalism as a way to liberate women. Marxist feminism states that private property, which gives rise to economic inequality, dependence, political confusion and ultimately unhealthy social relations between men and women, is the root of women's oppression.

According to Marxist theory, in capitalist societies the individual is shaped by class relations; that is, people's capacities, needs and interests are seen to be determined by the mode of production that characterises the society they inhabit. Marxist feminists see gender inequality as determined ultimately by the capitalist mode of production. Gender oppression is class oppression and women's subordination is seen as a form of class oppression which is maintained (like racism) because it serves the interests of capital and the ruling class. Marxist feminists have extended traditional Marxist analysis by looking at domestic labour as well as wage work in order to support their position.

❀ ❀ ❀

13

Marxism as a Political Practice

Since Marx's death in 1883, various groups around the world have appealed to Marxism as the theoretical basis for their politics and policies, which have often proved to be dramatically different and conflicting. One of the first major political splits occurred between the advocates of 'reformism,' who argued that the transition to socialism could occur within existing bourgeois parliamentarian frameworks, and communists, who argued that the transition to a socialist society required a revolution and the dissolution of the capitalist state. The 'reformist' tendency, later known as social democracy, came to be dominant in most of the parties affiliated to the Second International and these parties supported their own governments in the First World War. This issue caused the communists to break away, forming their own parties which became members of the Third International.

The following countries had governments at some point in the twentieth century who at least nominally adhered to Marxism: Albania, Afghanistan, Angola, Benin, Bulgaria, Chile, China, Republic of Congo, Cuba, Czechoslovakia, East Germany, Ethiopia, Grenada, Hungary, Laos, Moldova, Mongolia,

Mozambique, Nepal, Nicaragua, North Korea, Poland, Romania, Russia, the USSR and its republics, South Yemen, Yugoslavia, Venezuela, Vietnam. In addition, the Indian states of Kerala and West Bengal have had Marxist governments. Some of these governments such as in Venezuela, Nicaragua, Chile, Moldova and parts of India have been democratic in nature and maintained regular multiparty elections, while most governments claiming to be Marxist in nature have established authoritarian governments.

Marxist political parties and movements have significantly declined since the fall of the Soviet Union, with some exceptions, perhaps most notably Nepal.

History

The 1917 October Revolution, led by Vladimir Lenin, was the first large scale attempt to put Marxist ideas about a workers' state into practice. The new government faced counter-revolution, civil war and foreign intervention. Many, both inside and outside the revolution, worried that the revolution came too early in Russia's economic development. Consequently, the major Socialist Party in the UK decried the revolution as anti-Marxist within twenty-four hours, according to Jonathan Wolff. Lenin consistently explained "this elementary truth of Marxism, that the victory of socialism requires the joint efforts of workers in a number of advanced countries" (Lenin, Sochineniya (Works), 5th ed. Vol XLIV p418.) It could not be developed in Russia in isolation, he argued, but needed to be spread internationally. The 1917 October Revolution did help inspire a revolutionary wave over the years that followed, with the development of Communist Parties worldwide, but without success in the vital advanced capitalist countries of Western Europe. Socialist revolution in Germany and other western countries failed, leaving the Soviet Union on its own. An intense period of debate and stopgap solutions ensued, war communism and the New Economic Policy (NEP). Lenin died and Joseph Stalin gradually assumed control, eliminating rivals and consolidating power as the Soviet Union faced the events of the 1930s and its global crisis-tendencies. Amidst the geopolitical threats which defined the period and included the probability of invasion, he instituted a ruthless program of industrialisation which, while successful, was executed at great cost in human suffering, including millions of deaths, along with long-term environmental devastation.

Modern followers of Leon Trotsky maintain that as predicted by Lenin, Trotsky, and others already in the 1920s, Stalin's "socialism in one country" was unable to maintain itself, and according to some Marxist critics, the USSR ceased to show the characteristics of a socialist state long before its formal dissolution.

In the 1920s the economic calculation debate between Austrian Economists and Marxist economists took place. The Austrians claimed that Marxism is flawed because prices could not be set to recognize opportunity costs of factors of production, and so socialism could not make rational decisions.

Following World War II, Marxist ideology, often with Soviet military backing, spawned a rise in revolutionary communist parties all over the world. Some of these parties were eventually able to gain power, and establish their own version of a Marxist state. Such nations included the People's Republic of China, Vietnam, Romania, East Germany, Albania, Cambodia, Ethiopia, South Yemen, Yugoslavia, Cuba, and others. In some cases, these nations did not get along. The most notable examples were rifts that occurred between the Soviet Union and China, as well as Soviet Union and Yugoslavia (in 1948), whose leaders disagreed on certain elements of Marxism and how it should be implemented into society.

Many of these self-proclaimed Marxist nations (often styled People's Republics) eventually became authoritarian states, with stagnating economies. This caused some debate about whether Marxism was doomed in practise or these nations were in fact not led by "true Marxists". Critics of Marxism speculated that perhaps Marxist ideology itself was to blame for the nations' various problems. Followers of the currents within Marxism which opposed Stalin, principally cohered around Leon Trotsky and tended to locate the failure at the level of the failure of world revolution: for communism to have succeeded, they argue, it needed to encompass all the international trading relationships that capitalism had previously developed.

The Chinese experience seems to be unique. Rather than falling under a single family's self-serving and dynastic interpretation of Marxism as happened in North Korea and before 1989 in Eastern Europe, the Chinese government - after the end of the struggles over the Mao legacy in 1980 and the ascent of Deng Xiaoping - seems to have solved the succession crises that have plagued self-proclaimed Leninist governments since the death of Lenin himself. Key to this success is another Leninism which is a NEP (New Economic Policy) writ very large; Lenin's own NEP of the 1920s was the "permission" given to markets including speculation to operate by the Party which retained final control. The Russian experience in Perestroika was that markets under socialism were so opaque as to be both inefficient and corrupt but especially after China's application to join the WTO this does not seem to apply universally.

The death of "Marxism" in China has been prematurely announced but since the Hong Kong handover in 1997, the Beijing leadership has clearly retained final say over both commercial and political affairs. Questions remain however as to whether the Chinese Party has opened its markets to such a degree as to be no longer classified as a true Marxist party. A sort of tacit consent, and a desire in China's case to escape the chaos of pre-1949 memory, probably plays a role.

In 1991 the Soviet Union collapsed and the new Russian state ceased to identify itself with Marxism. Other nations around the world followed suit. Since then, radical Marxism or Communism has generally ceased to be a prominent political force in global politics, and has largely been replaced by more moderate versions of democratic socialism-or, more commonly, by neoliberal capitalism. Marxism has also had to engage with the rise in the Environmental movement. A merging of Marxism, socialism, ecology and environmentalism has been achieved, and is often referred to as Eco-socialism.

14

Social Democracy

Social democracy is a political ideology that emerged in the late 19th and early 20th century. Many parties in the second half of the 19th century described themselves as social democratic, such as the British Social Democratic Federation, and the Russian Social Democratic Labour Party. In most cases these were revolutionary socialist or Marxist groups, who were not only seeking to introduce socialism, but also democracy in un-democratic countries.

The modern social democratic current came into being through a break within the socialist movement in the early 20th century, between two groups holding different views on the ideas of Karl Marx. Many related movements, including pacifism, anarchism, and syndicalism, arose at the same time (often by splitting from the main socialist movement, but also by emerging of new theories.) and had various quite different objections to Marxism. The social democrats, who were the majority of socialists at this time, did not reject Marxism (and in fact claimed to uphold it), but wanted to *reform* it in certain ways and tone down their criticism of capitalism. They argued that socialism should be achieved through evolution rather than revolution. Such views were strongly opposed by the revolutionary socialists, who argued that any attempt to reform capitalism was doomed to fail, because the reformists would be gradually corrupted and eventually turn into capitalists themselves.

Despite their differences, the reformist and revolutionary branches of socialism remained united until the outbreak of World War I. The war proved to be the final straw that pushed the tensions between them to breaking point. The reformist socialists supported their respective national governments in the war, a fact that was seen by the revolutionary socialists as outright treason against the working class (Since it betrayed the principle that the workers "have no nation," and the fact that usually the lowest classes are the ones sent into the war to fight, and die, putting the cause at the side). Bitter arguments ensued within socialist parties, as for example between Eduard Bernstein (reformist socialist) and Rosa Luxemburg (revolutionary socialist) within the Social Democratic Party of Germany (SPD). Eventually, after the Russian Revolution of 1917, most of the world's socialist parties fractured. The reformist socialists kept the name "Social democrats," while the revolutionary socialists began calling themselves "Communists," and soon formed the modern Communist movement. (See also Comintern)

Since the 1920s, doctrinal differences have been constantly growing between social democrats and Communists (who themselves are not unified on the way to achieve socialism), and Social Democracy is mostly used as a specifically Central European label for Labour Parties since then, especially in Germany and the Netherlands and especially since the 1959 Godesberg Program of the German SPD that rejected the praxis of class struggle altogether.

Socialism

Although there are still many Marxist revolutionary social movements and political parties around the world, since the collapse of the Soviet Union and its satellite states, very few countries have governments which describe themselves as Marxist. Although socialistic parties are in power in some Western nations, they long ago distanced themselves from their direct link to Marx and his ideas.

As of 2007, Laos, Vietnam, Cuba, and the People's Republic of China - and to a certain extent Venezuela had governments in power which describe themselves as socialist in the Marxist sense. However, the private sector comprised more than 50% of the mainland Chinese economy by this time and the Vietnamese government had also partially liberalised its economy. The Laotian and Cuban states maintained strong control over the means of production.

Alexander Lukashenko president of Belarus, has been quoted as saying that his agrarian policy could be termed as Communist. He has also frequently referred to the economy as being 'market socialism.' Lukashenko is also an unapologetic admirer of the Soviet Union.

North Korea is another contemporary socialist state, though the official ideology of the Korean Workers' Party (originally led by Kim Il-sung and currently chaired by his son, Kim Jong-il), Juche, does not follow doctrinaire Marxism-Leninism as had been espoused by the leadership of the Soviet Union.

Libya is often thought of as a socialist state; it maintained ties with the Soviet Union and other Eastern bloc and Communist states during the Cold War. Colonel Muammar al-Gaddafi, the

Karl Marx

leader of Libya, describes the state's official ideology as Islamic socialism, and has labelled it a third way between capitalism and communism.

In the United Kingdom, the governing Labour Party used to describe itself as a socialist political party and is a member of the socialist organisation, Socialist International. The Party was set up by trade unionists, revolutionary and reformist socialists such as the Social Democratic Federation and the socialist Fabian Society.

15

Communism

Communist state is a term used by many political scientists to describe a form of government in which the state operates under a one-party system and declares allegiance to Marxism-Leninism or a derivative thereof. Communist states may have several legal political parties, but the Communist Party is constitutionally guaranteed a dominant role in government. Consequently, the institutions of the state and of the Communist Party become intimately entwined.

What separates Communist states from other one-party systems is the fact that ruling authorities in a Communist state refer to Marxism-Leninism as their guiding ideology. For Marxist-Leninists, the state and the Communist Party claim to act in accordance with the wishes of the industrial working class; for Maoists, the state and party claim to act in accordance to the peasantry. Both systems claim to have implemented a democratic dictatorship of the proletariat, and both claim to be moving towards the gradual abolition of the state and the implementation of communism. These claims have been strongly disputed by opponents of the historical Communist states, including communists who do not subscribe to Marxism-Leninism or who regard these states as bastardizations of the ideology.

Most Communist states adopted centrally planned economies. For this reason, Communist states are often associated with economic planning in both popular thought and scholarship. However, there are exceptions. The Soviet Union during the 1920s and Yugoslavia after World War II allowed limited markets and a degree of worker self-management. More recently, China and Vietnam have introduced far-reaching market reforms since the 1980s.

The policies adopted by Communist Parties ruling over communist states have been a source of political debate for much of the 20th century. However, this article describes the political structure of communist states, not the specific policies implemented by their governments.

Usage of the term

The term "communist state" originated in the West during the Cold War. It was coined to describe the form of government adopted by several countries in Eastern Europe and East Asia who followed the political model of the Soviet Union. These countries were ruled by parties which typically used the name "Communist Party of [country]." Since the separation of Party and State became very blurred in those countries, it seemed logical to name them "communist states" by analogy with the communist parties that ruled them.

Communists however dispute the validity of the term "communist state". In classical Marxism, communism is the final phase of history at which time the state would have "withered away" and therefore "communist state" is a contradiction in terms under premises of this theory. Current states are either in the capitalist or socialist phase of history - making the term "socialist state" preferable to Communists - and the role of the communist party (i.e. the vanguard party) is to pull a nation toward the communist phase of history. The reason why most Western scholars prefer the term "communist state" rather than "socialist state" to describe these countries is because most socialists oppose the idea of a vanguard party pulling a nation towards communism, and thus the term "socialist state" is liable to cause confusion.

Heterodox Marxists have also opposed the usage of the term "communist state." Since the 1930s, anti-Stalinist Marxists have argued that the existing communist states did not actually adhere to Marxism, but rather to a perversion of it that was heavily influenced by Stalinism. This critique was based on a variety of arguments, but nearly all anti-Stalinist communists argued that the Soviet model did not represent the interests of the working class. As such, Trotskyists referred to the Soviet Union as a "degenerated workers' state" and called its satellites "deformed workers states."

Not every country ruled by a communist party is viewed as a communist state. As noted above, the term "communist state" has been created and used by Western political scientists to refer to a specific type of one-party state. Communist parties have won elections and governed in the context of multi-party democracies, without seeking to establish a one-party state. Examples include Republic of Nicaragua (in the 1980s), Republic of Moldova (presently), Cyprus (presently), and the Indian states of Kerala, West Bengal and Tripura. These countries and states do not fall under the definition of a communist state.

State institutions

Communist states share similar institutions, which are organized on the premise that the communist party is a vanguard of the proletariat and represents the long-term interests of the people. The doctrine of democratic centralism, which was developed by Lenin as a set of principles to be used in the internal affairs of the communist party, is extended to society at large. According to democratic centralism, all leaders must be elected by the people and all proposals must be debated openly, but, once a decision has been reached, all people have a duty to obey that decision and all debate should end. When used within a political party, democratic centralism is meant to prevent factionalism and splits. When applied to an entire state, democratic centralism creates a one-party system.

The constitutions of most communist states describe their political system as a form of democracy. Thus, they recognize the sovereignty of the people as embodied in a series of representative parliamentary institutions. Communist states do not have a separation of powers; instead, they have one national legislative body (such as the Supreme Soviet in the Soviet Union) which is considered the highest organ of state power and which is legally superior to the executive and judicial branches of government. Such national legislative politics in communist states often have a similar structure to the parliaments that exist in liberal republics, with two significant differences: first, the deputies elected to these national legislative bodies are not expected to represent the interests of any particular constituency, but the long-term interests of the people as a whole; second, against Marx's advice, the legislative bodies of communist states are not in permanent session. Rather, they convene once or several times per year in sessions which usually last only a few days.

When the national legislative body is not in session - that is, most of the time - its powers are transferred to a smaller council (often called a "presidium") which combines legislative and executive power, and, in some communist states, acts as a collective head of state. The presidium is usually composed of important communist party members and votes the resolutions of the communist party into law.

Another feature of communist states is the existence of numerous state-sponsored social organizations (trade unions, youth organizations, women's organizations, associations of teachers, writers, journalists and other professionals, consumer cooperatives, sports clubs, etc.) which are integrated into the political system. In some communist states, representatives of these organizations are guaranteed a certain number of seats on the national legislative bodies. In all communist states, the social organizations are expected to promote social unity and cohesion, to serve as a link between the government and society, and to provide a forum for recruitment of new communist party members.

Communist states maintain their legitimacy by claiming to promote the long-term interests of the whole people, and communist parties justify their monopoly on political power by claiming to act in accordance with objective historical laws. Therefore, political opposition and dissent is regarded as counter-productive or even treasonous. Some communist states have more than one political party, but all minor parties are required to follow the leadership of the communist party. Criticism of proposed future policies is usually tolerated, as long as it does not turn into criticism of the political system itself. However, in accordance with the principles of democratic centralism, communist states usually do not tolerate criticism of policies that have already been implemented in the past or are being implemented in the present. However, communist states are widely seen as being *de facto* dictatorships by historians and sociologists, since the elections they held tended to be heavily rigged.

Criticism

Communist states have been criticized for their one-party dictatorships; totalitarian control of the economy and society; repression of civil liberties; economic focus on heavy industry at the expense of consumer goods, sometimes resulting in shortages of vital products or even famine; militarism; and propaganda to cover up the mistakes of the government. Communism itself does not necessarily advocate these actions, and this is one of the reasons why many communists regard communist states as bastardizations of communism.

List of current Communist states

The following countries are one-party states in which the ruling party declares allegiance to Marxism-Leninism and in which the institutions of the party and of the state have become intertwined; hence they fall under the definition of *Communist states*. They are listed here together with the year of their founding and their respective ruling parties.

- Countries where institutions of the communist party and state are intertwined:

- People's Republic of China (since 1949); Communist Party of China

- Republic of Cuba (Cuban Revolution in 1959, socialist state declared in 1961); Communist Party of Cuba

- Democratic People's Republic of Korea (since 1948); Korean Workers' Party

- Lao People's Democratic Republic (since 1975); Lao People's Revolutionary Party

- Socialist Republic of Vietnam (since 1976); Communist Party of Vietnam (ruled the Democratic Republic of Vietnam since 1954)

While these countries share a similar system of government, they have adopted very different economic policies over the past 15 years. For instance, the People's Republic of China has introduced sweeping market reforms. In addition, the various Communist states use different terms to identify themselves and their social systems. Laos has removed all references to Marxism-Leninism, communism and socialism in the Constitution in 1991. North Korea has removed references to Marxism-Leninism from its constitution and officially describes itself as following the ideology of Juche. Vietnam is "in transition toward socialism in the light of Marxism-Leninism" and Cuba is "a socialist state guided by ideas of Marx, Engels and Lenin and in transition to a communist society."

There are also three countries which currently have democratically elected communist parties heading the government. They are not one-party states and thus they do not fall under this article's definition of a Communist state:

- Cyprus, where the Progressive Party of Working People won the 2008 presidential election.

- Moldova, where the Party of Communists of the Republic of Moldova has governed the country since 2001.

- Nepal, where the Communist Party of Nepal (Maoist) has governed the country since 2008.

❁   ❁   ❁

Karl Marx

16

Marxism-Leninism

Marxism-Leninism, strictly speaking, refers to the version of Marxism developed by Vladimir Lenin known as Leninism. However, in various contexts, different (and sometimes opposing) political groups have used the term "Marxism-Leninism" to describe the ideologies that they claimed to be upholding. The core ideological features of Marxism-Leninism are those of Marxism and Leninism, that is to say, belief in the necessity of a violent overthrow of capitalism through communist revolution, to be followed by a dictatorship of the proletariat as the first stage of moving towards communism, and the need for a vanguard party to lead the proletariat in this effort. It involves subscribing to the teachings and legacy of Karl Marx and Friedrich Engels (Marxism), and that of Lenin, as carried forward by Joseph Stalin. Those who view themselves as Marxist-Leninists, however, vary with regards to the leaders and thinkers that they choose to uphold as progressive (and to what extent). Maoists tend to downplay the importance of all other thinkers in favour of Mao Zedong, whereas Hoxhaists repudiate Mao.

Leninism holds that capitalism can only be overthrown by revolutionary means; that is, any attempts to *reform* capitalism from within, such as Fabianism and non-revolutionary forms of democratic socialism, are doomed to fail. The first goal of a Leninist party is to educate the proletariat, so as to remove the various modes of false consciousness the bourgeois have instilled in them, instilled in order to make them more docile and easier to exploit economically, such as religion and nationalism. Once the proletariat has gained class consciousness the party will coordinate the proletariat's total might to overthrow the existing government, thus the proletariat will seize all political and economic power. Lastly the proletariat (thanks to their education by the party) will implement a dictatorship of the proletariat which would bring upon them socialism, the lower phase of communism. After this, the party would essentially dissolve as the entire proletariat is elevated to the level of revolutionaries.

The dictatorship of the proletariat refers to the absolute power of the working class. It is governed by a system of proletarian direct democracy; in which workers hold political power through local councils known as soviets.

Trotskyism

Trotskyism is the theory of Marxism as advocated by Leon Trotsky. Trotsky considered himself a Bolshevik-Leninist, arguing for the establishment of a vanguard party. He considered himself an advocate of orthodox Marxism. His politics differed sharply from those of Stalin or Mao, most importantly in declaring the need for an international "permanent revolution." Numerous groups around the world continue to describe themselves as Trotskyist and see themselves as standing in this tradition, although they have diverse interpretations of the conclusions to be drawn from this.

Trotsky advocated proletarian revolution as set out in his theory of "permanent revolution," and he argued that in countries where the bourgeois-democratic revolution had not triumphed already (in other words, in places that had not yet implemented a capitalist democracy, such as Russia before 1917), it was necessary that the proletariat make it permanent by carrying out the tasks of the social revolution (the "socialist" or "communist" revolution) at the same time, in an uninterrupted process. Trotsky believed that a new socialist state would not be able to hold out against the pressures of a hostile capitalist world unless socialist revolutions quickly took hold in other countries as well, especially in the industrial powers with a developed proletariat.

On the political spectrum of Marxism, Trotskyists are considered to be on the left. They fervently support democracy, oppose political deals with the imperialist powers, and advocate a spreading of the revolution until it becomes global.

Trotsky developed the theory that the Russian workers' state had become a "bureaucratically degenerated workers' state." Capitalist rule had not been restored, and nationalized industry and economic planning, instituted under Lenin, were still in effect. However, the state was controlled by a bureaucratic caste with interests hostile to those of the working class. Trotsky defended the Soviet Union against attack from imperialist powers and against internal counter-revolution, but called for a political revolution within the USSR to restore socialist democracy. He argued that if the working class did not take power away from the Stalinist bureaucracy, the bureaucracy would restore capitalism in order to enrich itself. In the view of many Trotskyists, this is exactly what has happened since the beginning of Glasnost and Perestroika in the USSR. Some argue that the adoption of market socialism by the People's Republic of China has also led to capitalist counter-revolution.

Maoism

Maoism, variably and officially known as Mao Zedong Thought is a variant of Marxism derived from the teachings of the late Chinese leader Mao Zedong (Wade-Giles Romanization: "Mao Tse-tung"), widely applied as the political and military guiding ideology in the Communist Party of China (CPC) from Mao's ascendancy to its leadership until the inception of Deng Xiaoping Theory and Chinese economic reforms in 1978. It is also applied internationally in contemporary times. Maoist parties and groups exist throughout the world, with notable groups in Peru, India, and Nepal, where they recently won the country's first free elections.

The basic tenets of Maoism include revolutionary struggle of the vast majority of people against what they term the exploiting classes and their state structures, termed a People's War. Usually involving peasants, its military strategies have involved guerrilla war tactics focused on surrounding the cities from the countryside, with a heavy emphasis on political transformation through the mass involvement of the basic people of the society. Maoism departs from conventional European-inspired Marxism in that its focus is on the agrarian countryside, rather than the industrial urban forces. Notably, successful Maoist parties in Peru, Nepal and Philippines have adopted equal stresses on urban and rural areas, depending on the country's level of development.

In its post-revolutionary period, Mao Zedong Thought is defined in the CPC's Constitution as "Marxism-Leninism applied in a Chinese context," synthesized by Mao Zedong and China's first-generation leaders. It asserts that class struggle continues even if the proletariat has already overthrown the bourgeoisie, and there are bourgeois restorationist elements within the Communist Party itself. It provided the CPC's first comprehensive theoretical guideline with regards to how to continue socialist revolution, the creation of a socialist society, socialist military construction, and highlights various contradictions in society to be addressed by what is termed "socialist construction." The ideology survives in name today on the Communist Party's Constitution; it is described as the guiding thought that created "new China" and a revolutionary concept against imperialism and feudalism.

Maoism broke with the state capitalist framework of the Soviet Union under Nikita Khrushchev and dismisses it as modern revisionism, a traditional pejorative term among communists referring to those who fight for capitalism in the name of socialism. Some critics claim that Maoists see Joseph Stalin as the last true socialist leader of the Soviet Union, although allowing the Maoist assessments of Stalin vary between the extremely positive and the more ambivalent. Whereas some political philosophers have seen in Maoism an attempt to combine Confucianism and Socialism - what one such called 'a third way between communism and capitalism.'

Maoism in China

Since the death of Mao Zedong in 1976, and the authoritarian capitalist reforms of Deng Xiaoping starting in 1978, the role of Mao's ideology within the PRC has radically changed. Although Mao Zedong Thought nominally remains the state ideology, Deng's admonition to seek truth from facts means that state policies are judged on their practical consequences and the role of ideology in determining policy has been considerably reduced.

Deng also separated Mao from Maoism, making it clear that Mao was fallible and hence th.t the truth of Maoism comes from observing social consequences rather than by using Mao's quotations as holy writ, as was done in Mao's lifetime.

In addition, the party constitution has been rewritten to give the authoritarian capitalist ideas of Deng Xiaoping prominence over those of Mao. One consequence of this is that groups outside China which describe themselves as Maoist generally regard China as having repudiated Maoism and restored capitalism, and there is a wide perception both in and out of China that China has abandoned Maoism. However, while it is now permissible to question particular actions of Mao and to talk about excesses taken in the name of Maoism, there is a prohibition in China on either publicly questioning the validity of Maoism or questioning whether the current actions of the CPC are "Maoist."

Although Mao Zedong Thought is still listed as one of the four cardinal principles of the People's Republic of China, its historical role has been re-assessed. The Communist Party now says that Maoism was necessary to break China free from its feudal past, but that the actions of Mao are seen to have led to excesses during the Cultural Revolution. The official view is that China has now reached an economic and political stage, known as the primary stage of socialism, in which China faces new and different problems completely unforeseen by Mao, and as such the solutions that Mao advocated are no longer relevant to China's current conditions. The official proclamation of the new CPC stand came in June 1981, when the Sixth Plenum of the Eleventh National Party Congress Central Committee took place. The 35,000-word "Resolution on Certain Questions in the History of Our Party Since the Founding of the People's Republic of China" reads:

"Chief responsibility for the grave `Left' error of the `cultural revolution, 'an error comprehensive in magnitude and protracted in duration, does indeed lie with Comrade Mao Zedong . . . . [and] far from making a correct analysis of many problems, he confused right and wrong and the people with the enemy. . . . Herein lies his tragedy."

Both Maoist critics outside China and most Western commentators see this re-working of the definition of Maoism as providing an ideological justification for what they see as the restoration of the essentials of capitalism in China by Deng and his successors.

Mao himself is officially regarded by the CPC as a "great revolutionary leader" for his role in fighting the Japanese and creating the People's Republic of China, but Maoism as implemented between 1959 and 1976 is regarded by today's CPC as an economic and political disaster. In Deng's day, support of radical Maoism was regarded as a form of "left deviationism" and being based on a cult of personality, although these 'errors' are officially attributed to the Gang of Four rather than to Mao himself. Thousands of Maoists were arrested in the Hua Guafeng period after 1976, with prominent Maoists sentenced to death.

These distinctions were very important in the early 1980s, when the Chinese government was faced with the dilemma of how to impose capitalism on a population that wasn't demanding it.

Debate within China

Many regret the erosion of guaranteed employment, education, health care, and other gains of the revolution that have been largely lost in the new profit-driven economy. This is reflected in a strain of

Chinese Neo-Leftism in the country that sees China's future in an advance towards socialism under changed conditions.

Some Western Marxist scholars argue that China's rapid industrialization and relatively quick recovery from the brutal period of civil wars 1911-1949 was a positive impact of Maoism, and contrast its development specifically to that of Southeast Asia, Russia and India. While others see it as catastrophe for the environment, with Maoism specifically engaged in a battle to dominate and subdue nature.

Maoism outside China

From 1962 onwards, the challenge to the Soviet hegemony in the World Communist Movement made by the CPC resulted in various divisions in communist parties around the world. At an early stage, the Albanian Party of Labour sided with the CPC. So did many of the mainstream (non-splinter group) communist parties in South-East Asia, like the Burmese Communist Party, Communist Party of Thailand, and Communist Party of Indonesia. Some Asian parties, like the Workers Party of Vietnam and the Workers Party of Korea attempted to take a middle-ground position.

In the west and south, a plethora of parties and organizations were formed that upheld links to the CPC. Often they took names such as *Communist Party (Marxist-Leninist)* or *Revolutionary Communist Party* to distinguish themselves from the traditional pro-Soviet communist parties. The pro-CPC movements were, in many cases, based amongst the wave of student radicalism that engulfed the world in the 1960s and 1970s.

Only one Western classic communist party sided with CPC, the Communist Party of New Zealand. Under the leadership of

CPC and Mao Zedong, a parallel international communist movement emerged to rival that of the Soviets, although it was never as formalized and homogeneous as the pro-Soviet tendency.

After the death of Mao in 1976 and the resulting power-struggles in China that followed, the international Maoist movement was divided into three camps. One group, composed of various ideologically non-aligned groups, gave weak support to the new Chinese leadership under Deng Xiaoping. Another camp denounced the new leadership as traitors to the cause of Marxism-Leninism-Mao Zedong Thought. The third camp sided with the Albanians in denouncing the Three Worlds Theory of the CPC (see Sino-Albanian Split.)

The pro-Albanian camp would start to function as an international group, led by Enver Hoxha and the APL, and was able to amalgamate many of the communist groups in Latin America, including the Communist Party of Brazil.

The new Chinese leadership showed little interest in the various foreign groups supporting Mao's China. Many of the foreign parties that were fraternal parties aligned with the Chinese government before 1975 either disbanded or abandoned the new Chinese government entirely, or even renounced Marxism-Leninism and developed into non-communist, social democratic parties. What is today called the "international Maoist movement" evolved out of the second camp - the parties that opposed Deng and claimed to uphold the legacy of Mao.

During the 1980s two parallel regrouping efforts emerged, one centered around the Communist Party of the Philippines, which gave birth to the ICMLPO, and one that birthed the Revolutionary Internationalist Movement, which the Shining Path communist guerrilla group and the Revolutionary Communist Party USA played a leading role in forming.

Both the International Conference and the RIM tendencies claimed to uphold Marxism-Leninism-Mao Zedong Thought, although RIM was later to substitute that ideology with what they termed 'Marxism-Leninism-Maoism.'

Maoism today

Today, Maoist organizations, grouped in RIM, have their greatest influence in South Asia. They have been involved in violent struggles in Bangladesh and, until recently, Nepal. The Nepalese Maoist militant struggles have ended and the Maoists have peacefully negotiated to become the majority party in the newly formed republic. There are also minor groups active in Afghanistan, Peru and Turkey.

In the Philippines, the Communist Party of the Philippines, which is not part of the RIM, leads an armed struggle through its military wing, the New People's Army.

In Peru, several columns of the Communist Party of Peru/SL are fighting a sporadic war. Since the capture of their leadership, Chairman Gonzalo and other members of their central committee in 1992, the PCP/SL no longer has initiative in the fight. Several different political positions are supported by the leadership of the PCP/SL.

In India, the Communist Party of India (Maoist) has been fighting a protracted war. Formed by the merger of the People's War Group and the Maoist Communist Centre ("notorious for its macabre killings") originating from the 25 May 1967 peasant uprising, they have expanded their range of operations to over half of India and have been listed by the Prime Minister as the "greatest internal security threat" to the Indian republic since it was founded.

In Germany, the ICMLPO-affiliated MLPD is the largest unambiguously-Marxist group in the country.

Maoism has also become a significant political ideology in Nepal. The Maoist insurgency has been fighting against the Royal Nepalese Army and other supporters of the monarchy. The Communist Party of Nepal (Maoist), a RIM member, has conditionally halted its armed struggle and is participating in an interim government, including in elections for a national assembly. True revolutionary Maoism appears doomed to extinction, however, with the rise of a powerful pro-Western faction of Chinese Communist Party apparatchiks in Peking, made affluent through the growth of global capitalism.

Military strategy

Mao is widely regarded in China as a brilliant military strategist even among those who oppose his political or economic ideas. His writings on guerrilla warfare, most notably in his groundbreaking primer *On Guerrilla Warfare*, and the notion of people's war are now generally considered to be essential reading, both for those who wish to conduct popular revolutions and for those who oppose them.

As with his economic and political ideas, Maoist military credo seems to have more relevance at the start of the 21st century outside of the People's Republic of China than within it. There is a consensus both within and outside the PRC that the military context that the PRC faces in the early 21st century are very different from the one faced by China in the 1930s. As a result, within the inner circle of the People's Liberation Army there has been extensive debate over whether and how to relate Mao's military doctrines to 21st-century military ideas, especially the idea of a revolution in military affairs.

Disputing these claims

Many academics dispute the claim that the above political movements are Marxist. Communist governments have historically been characterized by state ownership of productive resources in a planned economy and sweeping campaigns of economic restructuring such as nationalization of industry and land reform (often focusing on collective farming or state farms.) While they promote collective ownership of the means of production, Communist governments have been characterized by a strong state apparatus in which decisions are made by the ruling Communist Party. Dissident communists have characterized the Soviet model as state socialism or state capitalism. Further, critics have often claimed that a Stalinist or Maoist system of government creates a new ruling class, usually called the nomenklatura.

Marx defined "communism" as a classless, egalitarian and stateless society. To Marx, the notion of a communist state would have seemed an oxymoron, as he defined communism as the phase reached when class society and the state had already been abolished. Once the initial stage of socialism had been established, society would develop new social relations over the course of several generations, reaching what Marx called the higher phase of communism when bourgeois relations had been abandoned. Such a development has yet to occur in any historical self-claimed socialist state.

Some argue that socialist states have contained two new distinct classes: those who are in government and therefore have power, and those who are not in government and do not have

166   *Karl Marx*

power. Sometimes, this is taken to be a different form of capitalism, in which the government, as owner of the means of production, takes on the role formerly played by the bourgeois class; this arrangement is referred to as "State capitalism." These statist regimes have generally followed a command economy model without making a transition to this hypothetical final stage.

Criticisms

Criticisms of Marxism are many and varied. They concern both the theory itself, and its later interpretations and implementations.

Right

The Labour theory of value is no longer accepted by modern economists, with the ideas of marginal utility being used instead.

Marx and Engels never dedicated much work to show how exactly a communist economy would function, leaving Marxism, at least in its classical form, a "negative ideology, " concerned primarily with criticism of the status quo. Later generations of Marxists have attempted to fill in the gap, resulting in several different and competing Marxist views of the way a communist society should be organized.

Prominent economist Milton Friedman is of the opinion that free markets are the best and most efficient way of running the economy for the benefit of all. In the economic calculation debate between Austrian Economists and Marxist economists, the Austrians claimed that Marxism is flawed because prices could not be set to recognize opportunity costs of factors of production, and so socialism could not make rational decisions.

Individualists disagree with the basic approach of Marxism that of viewing all people as acting under the influence of socio-economic forces, and instead focus on the differences and unpredictable actions of individuals.

Left

Criticisms of Marxism have come from the political left as well as the political right:

- Democratic socialists and social democrats reject the idea that socialism can be accomplished only through class conflict and violent revolution.

- Many Anarchists reject the need for a transitory state phase on the road to a classless society.

Most thinkers on the left have rejected the fundamentals of Marxist theory, such as historical materialism and the labour theory of value, and gone on to criticize capitalism - and advocate socialism - using other arguments. Some contemporary supporters of Marxism argue that many aspects of Marxist thought are viable, but that the corpus also fails to deal effectively with certain aspects of economic, political or social theory.